HANDBOOK

OF THE

MEXICAN ARMY,

Prepared by the General Staff,
War Office

1906

The Naval & Military Press Ltd

Published by the
The Naval & Military Press

MILITARY HISTORY AT YOUR FINGERTIPS
www.naval-military-press.com

ONLINE GENEALOGY RESEARCH
www.military-genealogy.com

ONLINE MILITARY CARTOGRAPHY
www.militarymaproom.com

In reprinting in facsimile from the original, any imperfections are inevitably reproduced and the quality may fall short of modern type and cartographic standards.

PREFACE.

This Handbook replaces the short account of the Mexican Army given in Chapter I of the "Handbook of the Land Forces of the Central and South American Republics" issued by the General Staff in July, 1904. It has been compiled by Captain B. Atkinson, R.A. from information supplied for the most part by Colonel H. Foster, R.E., late Military Attaché, Washington. It has not been possible to obtain complete and reliable information in all cases, and therefore any additions or corrections will be gladly received.

J. M. GRIERSON,

Major General,

D.M.O.

GENERAL STAFF,

WAR OFFICE.

23rd February, 1906.

THE WAR OFFICE.
PRESIDENT.
SECRETARY OF WAR AND MARINE.
UNDER SECRETARY ("Oficial Major," who is in immediate charge of the Civil Side and in general charge of the working and discipline of the whole department.)
Civil Side.
Military Side.
Navy Department.
Secretariat.
Staff Departments.
Personal Office of Secretary. (Formulates desires and decisions of Secretary.)
Archives and Library Section. (In 3 sections—2 for Archives, 1 for Library.)
Bureau of Correspondence.
Bureau of the Registry.
Bureau of Finance.
Bureau of Telegrams.
Department of General Staff Corps.
Department of Cavalry. (In 2 sections and 4 boards.)
Department of Artillery. (In 4 sections:—1. Administration; 2. Armament and Ammunition; 3. Finance; 4. Library and Archives.)
Department of Engineers. (In 2 sections:—1. Tactical; 2. Technical, Organization, and Administration.)
Department of Infantry. (In 2 sections and 5 boards.)
Medical Department. (In 2 sections:—1. Medical; 2. Veterinary.)
1st Section. (Organization; distribution; mobilization; concentration; plans of campaign; intelligence; prisoners of war; spies; flags of truce; conventions; revision of regulations; auxiliary forces: National Guards, Rurales, and Police considered as Army Reserve: Staff, Engineer, and Artillery School.)
2nd Section. (Supreme War Council; correspondence with public and Government departments; posting and detail of officers; statistics as to personnel and matériel; formation of Staffs and of higher tactical units; Army List; record of services; school of military music; Military Invalids.)
3rd Section. (Secretary's reports; military law; courts martial; commissions; promotions; retirements; pensions; decorations; military prisons; police and martial law.)
4th Section. (Clothing; equipment; supply; remounts; requisitions for armament; war estimates; casualties; pensions to widows and orphans.)
5th Section. (Transport of troops; animals and wagons; railways; telegraphs; lines of communication in war.)
6th Section. (Library, maps, plans, lithography, photography, printing.)

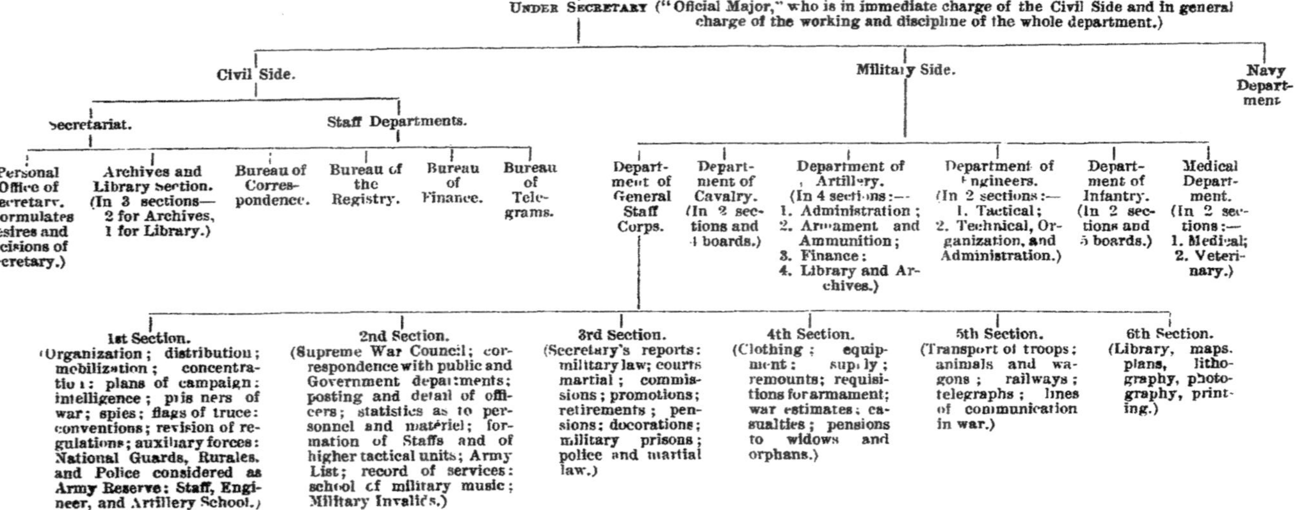

(8027)

INDEX.

PART I.

III.—Infantry.

IV.—Cavalry.

V.—Artillery.

VI.—Engineers.

VII.—Medical Department.

VIII.—Supply and Transport.

IX.—Military Police.

X.—First and Second Reserves.

XI.—Uniform.

PART II.

XII.—Interior Economy. Pay and Pension.

XIII.—Manufacturing Establishments. Warlike Stores.

XIV.—Education.

XV.—Military Law.

Appendix A.

Appendix B.

Appendix C.

HANDBOOK

OF THE

MEXICAN ARMY.

I. GOVERNMENT. WAR DEPARTMENT.

MEXICO is a Federative Republic formed by the union of 27 States, of 3 Territories controlled by the Federal Government, and of a Federal District which contains the capital.

Area.—With an area of some 767,000 square miles, it is as large as France, Germany, Austria and Italy.

Population.—Of the population of over 14 millions, some 19 per cent. are of pure, or of nearly pure, white race, 43 per cent. are of mixed race, and the remaining 38 per cent. are Indians. In 1900 the foreign population numbered 57,511. It included 16,000 Spaniards, 15,000 Americans, 5,000 Guatemalans, nearly 4,000 French and smaller numbers of English, Germans, Italians and Chinese.

Spanish is the official language.

GOVERNMENT.

By the constitution of 1857 the several States are free and sovereign in everything relating to their internal administration, but all real control and power is in the hands of the Federal or Supreme Government at the capital.

The legislative power of the nation is vested in a general Congress consisting of two Chambers, the Deputies and the Senate. The Chamber of Deputies is composed of representatives of the nation elected every two years by popular vote. Their number, which in 1897 amounted to 227, is limited to the proportion of 1 for every 40,000 inhabitants and for each fraction of over 20,000. The Senate consists at present of 56 members, 2 for each State and 2 for the Federal District. They are elected similarly to the Deputies, but their term of office is 4 years, half their number being renewed biennially.*

The executive power is entrusted to a single individual known as the "President of the United Mexican States." He is chosen indirectly by a body of electors nominated by the people. His term of office is 6 years and commences on the 1st day of the December following the election. He may be reelected indefinitely.† During his absence, or in the event of his death, his place is taken by the Vice-President who is elected for the same term and in a similar manner.

The President is assisted by a Cabinet consisting of 8 Secretaries of State—for Foreign Affairs, Interior, Justice, Public Instruction and the Fine Arts, Colonization and Industries, Communications and Public Works, Finance, and War and Marine.

The judicial power is vested in the Supreme Court of Justice and in the district and circuit courts. Of the latter there are 3 and 32 respectively. The

---

* "Mexico," International Bureau of the American Republics, 1904.

† Thus, General Porfirio Diaz, to whom the present prosperity of the country is due, was first elected in 1877 and, with the exception of a single term, has continued in office until the present day.

Supreme Court consists of 15 "ministros" or justices, an Attorney-General and a Public Prosecutor.

Their term of office is one of 6 years and they are elected similarly to the Deputies and Senators.

Government Control of Army.—Turning to matters more nearly military, the President commands both the army and the navy. He directs the patronage of both services and has the final word in all matters affecting their training, organisation and equipment. In time of war he assumes entire control of them and also of the National Guards of the several States. He presides over the Supreme Council of War, which consists of 5 generals—one of them acting as secretary—and which is charged with the confidential consideration of all military matters laid before it by the Government. His usual channel is the Secretary of War and Marine, who presides over the Supreme Council in his absence. This gentleman is assisted by an Under-Secretary, known as the "Oficial Mayor," who plays an important part in the administration of the war office.

In Congress is vested the power to approve treaties; to raise and maintain the army and navy; to consent to a declaration of war by the President; and to permit foreign allies to enter, and national troops to leave the country. Congress also lays down the regulations for the organization, armament, and discipline of the National Guards of the several States, but these States carry out the instruction of their troops and the National Guards appoint their own officers.

War Department.

Under the President, the Secretary of War and Marine is the head of the war department. The organization of this latter is shown in the following table. Each branch is under a general or a colonel, who has to assist him a staff of officers, and of clerks holding military rank.

General Staff.—A General of Brigade is at the head of the general staff. According to the law of October 31st, 1900, his staff—including the officers attached to the zones and commands—should consist of—

2 Colonels (assistant chiefs of the department).
4 Colonels.
8 Lieutenant-colonels.
15 Majors.
24 First-captains.
2 Majors of Cavalry (attached).
A variable number of Second-captains and Lieutenants.

In September, 1905, the numbers actually employed in the department were—

4 Colonels.
4 Lieutenant-colonels.
10 Majors.
34 Captains.
6 Lieutenants.

At present, appointment to this body is confined to those officers who have concluded the course of study for staff employment at the military college, and to regimental officers who show especial promise and who have passed a qualifying examination. As a rule, every officer entering the general staff spends 6 months on the military side of the war department. Thence he passes to regimental duty, and finally to the general staff and to the geographical commissions. The Chief of the General Staff regulates the duration of his appointment, and advises the Secretary of War when changes become necessary.*

* Reglamento del Cuerpo Especial de Estado Major, 1900.

President's Staff.—The President also has a small staff of his own. It consists of a general or colonel as chief, and of 4 aides-de-camp selected, 1 from the engineers or the navy, 1 from the general staff, 1 from the artillery, and 1 from the cavalry or infantry. There are also 4 orderly officers, chosen from the arms selected by the President. Its real function is that of a small and select bodyguard. It is little more than a paper organization and, at the present moment, some of the posts are filled by civilians with honorary rank. The Secretary of War also has a similar staff of 5 officers.*

II.—RECRUITMENT. PEACE AND WAR ORGANIZATIONS.

Recruitment.

The military forces consist of :—

1. The Standing Army.
2. The First Reserve.
3. The Second Reserve.

The standing army is limited to 30,000 men, and consists at present of about 28,000.

Men.—The conditions of enlistment are that the man must† :—

(*a*) Be between 18 and 45 years of age.
(*b*) Be Mexican by birth or by naturalization.
(*c*) Not have lost his rights of citizenship by imprisonment.
(*d*) Be physically and intellectually sound.
(*e*) Understand the Spanish language.

* Captain Garcia y Pérez's Report to the Spanish Government, 1902.
† "Codigo Militar," 1900.

The term of enlistment is for 3, 4, or 5 years, and the man may re-engage for periods of 4 years.

Theoretically, the army is a voluntary one. Practically, sufficient numbers of recruits are never forthcoming and the Government is forced to make up the deficiency by annual compulsory contingents levied from the separate States. These contingents are obtained by ballot, but, by reason of exemption and substitution, the lot falls upon the lowest classes of society. Military service may be inflicted as a punishment for minor criminal offences.

The only true volunteers are the President's body-guard, the engineers, the military police, the drivers of the artillery and of the train, and the men of a few cavalry and infantry regiments which secure recruits by reason of the personal popularity of their officers.

A scheme embodying compulsory military service has been considered. It has been postponed for the present.

Even under existing conditions, every male citizen between the ages of 18 and 50 is liable to service in time of war.

The rank and file of the army are of the native Indian race.

Officers.—The officers are of Spanish or of mixed descent.

Up to the present time they have been obtained from* :—

1. The Military College at Chapultepec.
2. The promotion of sergeants from the ranks.
3. The State National Guards.
4. The bandsmen of the Military College.
5. Civilian sources.†

---

* Message of Secretary of War to Congress, 1904.

† Certain departments, such as that of Pay and Supply, are officered almost entirely by civilians with military rank.

In the words of the Secretary of War, this great variety of sources has proved extremely prejudicial to efficiency and to discipline. Only the first-named—the military college—provides any real military education and it, intended primarily for the training of the staff and scientific branches, furnishes but a limited number of officers to the fighting arms—the cavalry, the artillery and the infantry.

To remedy this defect, the "Escuela de Aspirantes" (p. 89) was established in 1905 and in future no person who has not passed either through it or through the military college will be granted a commission in the army. And furthermore, all officers below the rank of major now serving in the army are required to undergo a course of instruction at the "Escuela de Aspirantes" unless they were originally commissioned from the military college.

Promotion up to the rank of field officer is by examination and depends upon the favourable report of the commanding officer. It is generally by seniority but may be by selection. In the higher ranks military knowledge is taken for granted and promotion is by seniority tempered with a certain amount of elimination. Retirement is compulsory at the following ages* :—

General of Brigade	66
Brigadier...	65
Colonel	60
Lieutenant-colonel	56
Major	52
Captain	48
Lieutenant	46

First Reserve.—The first reserve consists of :—

(*a*) Army officers on the reserve list.

* "Ley Organica," 1900.

(*b*) The Rural and Urban Police of the Federation and of the States.

(*c*) The Fiscal Police and the Coast and Frontier Guards.

These form a trained and disciplined force of some 20,000 men.

Second Reserve.—The second reserve consists of the National Guards of the several States. It is an untrained badly-equipped force of under 20,000 men. It will probably be allowed to die out.

Peace Organization.

The standing army consists of :—

26 Battalions of Infantry of the Line.
4 Cadre-battalions of Infantry.
2 Regional Battalions of Infantry.
2 Regional Companies of Infantry.
14 Regiments of Cavalry of the Line.
4 Cadre-regiments of Cavalry.
2 Regiments of Field Artillery.
1 Regiment of Horse Artillery.
1 Regiment of Mountain Artillery.
1 Machine Gun Company.
1 Squadron of Light Artillery with Q.F. guns for use with Cavalry.
2 Sections of Artillery Train.
4 Detachments of Fortress Artillery.
1 Battalion of Sappers.
1 Engineer Park.
1 Bridging Train.
1 Telegraph Section.
1 Transport Squadron.
1 Squadron of Military Police.
1 Company of Hospital Orderlies.
1 Ambulance Train.

Present Strength :—

Generals of Division ...	8	
" Brigade ...	54	
Brigadiers	48	
Field Officers	758	
Junior Officers	2,526	
Total	——	3,394
N.C.O.'s and Men... ...		24,785
Grand Total		28,179
Horses		6,683
Mules		2,765

Or, distributed by arms :—

Infantry	16,000
Cavalry	7,000
Artillery	1,900
Engineers	600
Other arms	2,500
	28,000

In time of peace there are no units larger than regiments or battalions.

It will be noticed in the following chapters that their organization is uniform and symmetrical. Each regiment or battalion is subdivided into 4 squadrons, companies, or batteries, and in each instance the regimental staffs are practically identical. Where there are drivers, they have their own separate non-commissioned officers.

Zones.—These units are scattered over 10 military zones, and over a few minor commands known as "Comandancias" and as "Jefaturas."

The first zone comprises the States of Sonora, Sinaloa, and the territory of Lower California. Headquarters at Hermosillo.

The second zone comprises the States of Durango and Chihuahua. Headquarters at the town of Chihuahua.

The third zone comprises the States of Coahuila, Tamaulipas, and Nuevo León. Headquarters at Monterey.

The fourth zone comprises the States of Jalisco and Colima, and the territory of Tepic. Headquarters at Guadalajara.

The fifth zone comprises the States of San Luis Potosí, Zacatecas, and Aguascalientes. Headquarters at San Luis Potosí.

The sixth zone comprises the States of Michoacán, Querétaro, and Guanajuato. Headquarters at León.

The seventh zone comprises the States of Puebla, Guerrero, Tlaxcala, and Vera Cruz. Headquarters at Puebla.

The eighth zone comprises the State of Oaxaca, with the exception of the districts of Juchitán and Tehuantepec. Headquarters at Oaxaca.

The ninth zone comprises the State of Chiapas and the districts of Juchitan and Tehuantepec in Oaxaca, and of Minatitlan in Vera Cruz. Headquarters at Juchitan.

The tenth zone comprises the States of Tabasco, Campeche, and Yucatan. Headquarters at Merida.

Each zone is commanded by a colonel or brigadier, with a staff of 3 officers. He is under the immediate orders of the war department.

The first "Comandancia" comprises the States of Mexico, Hidalgo and Morelos, and the Federal district. This command is concentrated in the capital and is by far the most important, for it includes the whole of the artillery, engineers, and special corps, and also several regiments of cavalry and infantry.

The second comandancia is that of Vera Cruz, the third is that of Acapulco.

The Jefaturas are smaller commands at Tampico and Torreon, in the frontier cities of Matamoros and Ciudad Juarez, in the states of Michoacan, Guerrero, Sinaloa, Tabasco, and Campeche, and in the territories of Lower California, Tepic, and Quintana Roo.

Distribution on July 31st, 1905 :—*

Federal District	...	4 Regiments Cavalry.
"	...	All the artillery, engineers, and special corps.
"	...	6 Battalions Infantry.
Morelia ...	...	1 Battalion Infantry.
Sonora ...	...	2 Regiments Cavalry.
" ...	...	4 Battalions Infantry.
Puebla ...	...	1 Regiment Cavalry.
" ...	...	1 Cadre-regiment Cavalry.
" ...	...	2 Battalions Infantry.
Oaxaca ...	...	1 Regiment Cavalry.
" ...	...	2 Battalions Infantry.
Vera Cruz ...	...	3 Battalions Infantry.
Nuevo León	...	1 Regiment Cavalry.
"	...	2 Battalions Infantry.
Jalisco ...	...	1 Regiment Cavalry.
" ...	...	1 Battalion Infantry.
Quintana Roo	...	1 Battalion Infantry.
"	...	2 Regional Battalions Infantry.
Sinaloa ...	...	1 Battalion Infantry.
San Luis Potosí	...	1 Battalion Infantry.
Chihuahua ...	...	1 Battalion Infantry.
Guanajuato	...	2 Regiments Cavalry.
Tamaulipas...	...	1 Cadre-regiment Cavalry.
" ...	...	2 Cadre-battalions Infantry.
Tepic ...	...	1 Cadre-battalion Infantry.
Campeche ...	...	1 Cadre-battalion Infantry.
Mexico ...	...	2 Regiments Cavalry.

* "Diario Oficial, Estados Unidos Mexicanos." This distribution list is not quite accurate for the "Diario" stations the 4th Regiment of Cavalry both in Mexico and Puebla, while it omits altogether the 6th Regiment of Infantry.

Coahuila	1 Regiment Cavalry.
"	1 Cadre-regiment Cavalry.
Zacatecas	1 Cadre-regiment Cavalry.
Lower California ...	2 Regional Companies.

In addition to the above, there were corps of auxiliaries* in Puebla and in Sonora.

War Organization.

In time of war these troops are to be organized in brigades, divisions and army corps, for which establishments are laid down. Provision is also made for the formation of their staffs. But it must be remembered that the Mexican army has never been mobilized under these conditions and that it is doubtful if the following organizations ever could be or would be adopted. This remark applies with almost equal force to the mobilization of the various units.

A brigade is to be composed of from 2 to 4 battalions of infantry, or from 2 to 4 regiments of cavalry. The combination of 2 battalions of infantry and a regiment of cavalry, or 2 regiments of cavalry and a battalion of infantry, is called a mixed brigade. A force consisting of more than 1 regiment or battalion, but smaller than a brigade, is called a "section" (*seccion*), and the combination of fractions of the three arms is called a "mixed section."

A division is to be composed of from 2 to 4 brigades of infantry or from 2 to 4 brigades of cavalry, while the union of 2 brigades of infantry and 1 of cavalry, or of 2 brigades of cavalry and 1 of infantry is called a mixed division. An army corps is to be composed of 3 divisions, but may contain either 2 or 4 of these units.

---

* The term "auxiliary" is applied to the National Guards and to forces raised temporarily for the suppression of small disturbances such as the Maya rising.

To brigades, divisions, and army corps is added such a proportion of artillery, engineers, medical corps, train, military police, and other services as the Secretary of War may determine.

The composition of a brigade acting independently is* :—

Staff (staff of an infantry brigade [*see* below], with half the personnel of a divisional staff).
1 Regiment Cavalry.
2 Batteries Field Artillery.
2 Batteries Light Artillery.
1 Group of 4 light Q.F. guns.
1 Bridging Section.
2 Regiments Infantry with a brigade staff.
1 Divisional Artillery Park.
1 „ Engineer „
1 Ambulance Section.
1 Field Hospital.
1 Half-troop Military Police.
1 Squad of Telegraphists.
1 Supply Column of varying size.

Total strength, about 5,000.

A normal division consists of :—

Staff. (*See* below.)
2 Infantry Brigades, each of 2 regiments of 2 battalions.
1 Cavalry Brigade of 2 regiments, each of 6 squadrons.†
4 Field or Mountain Batteries.
1 Detachment of light Q.F. guns.
A variable number of machine guns.
1 Engineer Company.
1 Divisional Artillery Park.
1 „ Engineer „
1 Telegraph Company.

---

* Captain Garcia y Pérez's report.

† The "Ley Organica" states that a group of 8 Q.F. guns is to be attached to the cavalry brigade.

1 Troop Military Police.
1 Bearer Company.
1 Field Hospital.
1 Supply Column, carrying rations for 4 days in addition to the amounts carried by the units.

Total strength, about 500 officers and 10,000 men.

The staff of an infantry brigade forming part of a division is :—*

1 General of Brigade or Brigadier.
1 Lieutenant-colonel or Major of the General Staff.
1 Lieutenant of Cavalry as A.D.C.
1 Lieutenant of the General Staff.
5 Orderlies.
2 Teamsters.
1 Bugler.
1 Half-troop of Divisional Cavalry as escort.

The staff of a cavalry brigade forming part of an infantry division is :—*

1 Brigadier or Colonel.
1 Lieutenant-colonel of the General Staff.
1 Captain of Cavalry.
2 Lieutenants of Cavalry.
1 Lieutenant of the General Staff.
6 Orderlies.
2 Teamsters.
1 Trumpeter.
1 Half-troop as escort.

The staff of a normal infantry division is :—*

Headquarters Staff—

1 General, Commanding.
1 Colonel of the General Staff.
1 Major " " "

* "Ley Organica," 1900.

1 First-captain of the General Staff.
2 Lieutenants „ „ „
3 Clerks.

Artillery—

1 Colonel, Commanding.
1 Second-captain of Artillery.
1 Lieutenant of „

Engineers—

1 Colonel, Commanding.
1 First-captain of Engineers.
1 Lieutenant „

Medical—

1 Surgeon-colonel, Commanding.
1 Surgeon-major.
1 Veterinary Major or Captain.
1 Veterinary Sergeant.

Supplies—

1 Divisional Paymaster.
2 Paymasters.

Provost—

1 Major of Cavalry, Provost-Marshal.
1 Legal Assessor.
1 Lieutenant of Cavalry, clerk to Provost-Marshal.
1 Lieutenant of Cavalry, clerk to Assessor.

Transport—

1 Major of Cavalry, baggage-master.
1 Lieutenant of Cavalry, adjutant.

Escort—

1 Lieutenant, Commanding.
1 Second-sergeant.
1 Corporal-trumpeter.
2 Corporals.
14 Troopers.

25 Mounted Orderlies, who march with the escort, but are allotted as follows :—Headquarters Staff, 9 ; Artillery, 3 ; Engineers, 3 ; Supply, 3 ; Provost, 4.

Total strength, 72.

The staff of an army corps is :—*

Headquarters Staff—

1 General of Brigade.
1 Brigadier or Colonel of the General Staff.
1 Lieutenant-colonel or Major of the General Staff.
2 First-captains of the General Staff.
2 Second-captains of the General Staff.
2 Lieutenants of the General Staff.
1 Major of Cavalry, Camp Commandant.
1 Lieutenant of Cavalry.
3 Clerks.
25 Orderlies.
2 Extra Orderlies for the Chief of the Staff.
4 Teamsters.
12 Pack mules.
4 Saddle mules.

Artillery—

1 Colonel, Commanding.
1 First-captain of Artillery.
1 Second-captain of Artillery.
2 Lieutenants "
5 Cavalry Orderlies.
2 Teamsters.

Engineers—

1 Colonel, Commanding.
1 First-captain of Engineers.
1 Second-captain of Engineers.

* "Reglamento del Cuerpo Especial de Estado Major," 1900.

2 Lieutenants of Engineers.
5 Cavalry Orderlies.
2 Teamsters.
5 Pack and Saddle mules.

Medical—

1 Surgeon-colonel, Commanding.
2 Surgeon-captains.
1 Veterinary First-captain.
1 First-captain, apothecary.
2 Artificers.
5 Cavalry Orderlies.
2 Teamsters.
9 Mules.

Supplies—

1 Army Corps Paymaster.
3 Regimental Paymasters.
3 Paymasters.
7 Cavalry Orderlies.
6 Teamsters.
18 Mules.

(This section is in charge of the army corps transport train.)

Provost—

1 Lieutenant-colonel of Cavalry, Provost-Marshal.
1 Second-lieutenant of Cavalry, Adjutant.
1 Legal Assessor.
1 Lieutenant of Cavalry, clerk to assessor.
1 Second-captain of Military Police.
2 Troops of Military Police.
3 Cavalry Orderlies.
2 Teamsters.

Expansion of the Units. As the present peace establishment is manifestly insufficient to provide even a reasonable number of the larger units, the following increases are arranged to take place upon the mobilization of the army :—

Cavalry.—Each regiment forms 2 additional squadrons, making 6 squadrons in all. Each cadre regiment becomes a regiment on the higher peace establishment.

Horse Artillery.—The regiment forms 2 additional batteries, or six 4-gun batteries in all.

Field and Mountain Artillery.—Each regiment doubles the number of its batteries.

Light Artillery.—The squadron is doubled.

Machine Gun Company.—The strength is doubled.

Artillery Train.—Expands into the necessary number of divisional ammunition columns.

Engineers.—The battalion is increased to provide 1 company for each division. The bridging train is almost doubled. New telegraph and railway companies are formed from Goverment employés.

Infantry.—Each battalion forms a regiment of 2 battalions. Each cadre and regional battalion, and each regional company, becomes a battalion at war strength.

Medical Services.—Sufficient bearer companies and field hospitals are formed to enable 1 of each to be allotted to every division.

Transport.—The necessary number of columns is raised.

Military Police.—The necessary number of squadrons is raised.

This expansion is somewhat simplified by the very large proportion of officers—1 to every 7 or 8 men—maintained in time of peace. The existing infantry and cavalry would supply the artillery with the necessary gunners and drivers.

Old soldiers would be re-enlisted, the National Guards would be incorporated in the army, as also the entire police force of the Republic, including the Rurales, the Federal and the State Police, the Fiscal Police and the Coast and Frontier Guards.

Additional officers could be obtained from the reserve, which includes all officers unemployed in time of peace.

The field army may therefore consist of* :—

Staff		400
Cavalry—		
14 Regiments, each 836	11,704	
4 Cadre regiments, each 619	2,476	
		14,180
Artillery—		
6 Horse batteries, each 76	456	
" staff...	14	
16 Field batteries, each 127	1,932	
" staff	14	
8 Mountain batteries, each 122	976	
" staff	15	
2 Light squadrons, each 148	296	
" staff	6	
4 Machine gun divisions, each 75	300	
" " staff	14	
4 ammunition columns, each 179	716	
		4.739
Engineers—		
1 Battalion, 4 companies, each 189	756	
" staff...	27	
1 Park	23	
1 Bridging train...	173	
4 Telegraph companies, each 131	524	
		1,503
Infantry—		
52 Battalions, each 937	48,724	
4 Cadre battalions, each 937	3,748	
2 Regional battalions, each 937	1,874	
2 Regional companies, each 937	1,874	
		56,220
Medical Dept.—		
4 Bearer companies, each 100	400	
4 Field hospitals, each 208	832	
		1,232
Supply—		
16 Companies, each 67		1,072
Military Police—		
2 Squadrons, each 121		242
Total		79,588

* The following figures do not pretend to be accurate, they are merely a summary of the following chapters.

Or, in round numbers—

80,000 men.
200 field guns.
48 machine guns.
20,000 horses.
10,000 mules.

III.—INFANTRY.

The infantry is divided into:—

26 Battalions.
4 Cadre-battalions.
2 Regional Battalions.
2 Regional Companies.

Battalion.

Organization.—The battalion consists of 4 companies, each divided into 3 sections. Each section is divided into 2 half-sections (peloton), and the half-section into 3 squads (escuadra). The squad is commanded by a corporal, and from it a smart man and good shot is chosen to be trained as scout. When the company scouts work independently they are commanded by a sergeant and by 2 corporals selected by the company commander. But when the scouts of the battalion work together they are commanded by a second-captain and by 2 subalterns selected by the commanding officer. These men receive 1 dollar per month extra pay.

Mobilization.—On mobilization each battalion doubles its strength and forms a regiment of 2 battalions. The lieutenant-colonel takes command of the second battalion, whose companies are handed over to the second-captains. The 4 additional subalterns are obtained from the pay department, or from the military college, or by promoting first-sergeants. The supernumerary 8 sergeants and 4 corporals join the second battalion, and 16 sergeants, 16 corporals, and 16 men are promoted to complete the establishment; 20 old soldiers per company also join the second battalion to form a nucleus of trained men.

Regimental Staff.

Personnel.	Higher and Lower Peace Establishments.	War Establishment.	
		1st Battalion.	2nd Battalion.
Colonel	1	1	—
Lieutenant-colonel	1	—	1
Major	1	1	—
First-captain, adjutant ...	1	—	1
Second-captain, paymaster	1	1	—
Lieutenant, adjutant ...	—	—	1
Second-lieutenants, assistant-adjutants	2	1	1
First-sergeant, bugler ...	1	1	—
Sergeant, bugler	1	—	1
Corporal, bugler	1	1	1
Sergeants, clerks	2	1	1
Corporals	8	2	2
Artificer, armourer ...	1	1	—
Corporal of teamsters ...	1	1	2
Teamsters	6 or 9*	10	10
Total	28 or 31*	21	21
Mules	10 or 29*	33	33

* The double sets of figures refer to the higher and lower establishments.

Company.

Personnel.	Higher and Lower Peace Establishments.	War Establishment.
First-captain	1	1
Second-captain	1	
Lieutenants	3	2
Lieutenant, paymaster	1	—
Second-lieutenants	3	2
First-sergeant	1	1
Sergeant, assistant-first-sergeant...	1	1
Sergeants	18	6
Corporals	8	18
Corporal, standard-bearer... ...	1	1
,, of teamsters	—	1
Buglers	6	4
Drummers	—	2
Privates	110 or 190*†	190†
Total	154 or 234*	229
Mules	7	6

* The double sets of figures refer to the higher and lower establishments.

The following numbers are detailed from the privates :—

	Lower Peace Establishment.	Higher Peace Establishment.	War Establishment.
Teamsters	3	6	6
Stretcher bearers ...	4	4	4
Officers' servants, &c....	8	8	6

The strength of a battalion is, therefore, as under :—

Unit.	Officers.	Men.	Mules.
Regimental staff	4	17	33
4 companies	20	896	24
Total	24	91	57

CADRE-BATTALION.

The 4 cadre-battalions may be either "in cadre" or on the lower peace establishment. In the latter case they are identical with a line regiment on the same establishment.

When in cadre, the regimental staff consists of :—

1 Lieutenant-colonel.
1 Major.
1 Second-captain, adjutant.
1 Sergeant, bugler.
1 Corporal, bugler.
1 Artificer, armourer.
1 Corporal, teamster.
3 Teamsters.
—
10, with 6 mules.

In cadre again, the battalion consists of only 2 companies, each with the following establishment :—

1 Second-captain.
1 Lieutenant.
2 Second-lieutenants.
1 First-sergeant.
1 Sergeant, assistant-first-sergeant.
3 Sergeants.
9 Corporals.
3 Buglers.
*54 Privates.
—
75, with 5 mules.

The company is divided into 9 squads, from each of which a selected man is trained as a scout, and receives 1 dollar per month extra pay.

On mobilization the cadre-battalions are raised in succession to the lower and higher peace establishments, and finally become battalions at war strength.

Regional Battalion.

The two regional battalions are maintained on the lower peace establishment of regiments of the line. On mobilization they are brought up to the battalion war strength. They are generally stationed in Quintana Roo and the two regional companies in Lower California.

* 2 privates are employed as teamsters, 2 as stretcher-bearers, and 3 as officers' servants, &c.

The establishment of the company is :—

1 First-captain.
1 Second-captain.
3 Lieutenants.
1 First-sergeant.
7 Sergeants.
18 Corporals.
6 Buglers.
*108 Privates.
2 Teamsters.

147, with 10 mules.

On mobilization they become battalions at war strength.

Armament.—The infantry are armed with the 7 mm. (·275-inch) Mauser rifle.† They carry a bayonet in a sheath hanging from the waist-belt. It is generally fixed at drill and on the march.

Equipment.—A square cartridge-box is slung over the left shoulder. The 14-inch square knapsack is of thin wood, covered with canvas. It has wooden partitions for brushes, food and linen. The greatcoat is carried in a roll round the top and sides of the knapsack. To the rear face is attached a block-tin water-bottle. A square drinking cup fits over the end, and it is enclosed in 2 deep square cooking utensils with folding wire handles.

Each corporal and private carries an entrenching tool.‡

Each company is equipped with 8 shovels, 4 picks, 2 choppers (machete), 1 hand-axe, 1 jointed saw, and 2 crowbars. The saw and the crowbars are carried on one of the pack-mules, the remainder by the men.

* 3 privates are employed as teamsters, 4 as stretcher-bearers, and 5 as officers' servants, &c.

† It is possible that this rifle may be replaced by the 7-mm. Mondragon semi-automatic rifle. This weighs 9 lbs. 10 oz., and has a muzzle velocity of 2,149 f.s. It can be used as an ordinary magazine rifle.

‡ "Ley Organica del Ejercito Nacional," 1900.

Ammunition.—The amount of ammunition carried is :—*

On the man	... ...	150 rounds.
Company mules ...	...	40 „
Battalion reserve	...	40 „
Ammunition column	...	64 „
Total	... ...	294 „

Musketry practice is carried out once a month in every battalion, and every soldier fires annually 65 rounds of ball cartridge.†

Uniform.—The uniform and distinctive marks are described in page 76.

IV.—CAVALRY.

There is only one class of regular cavalry. It is divided into 14 regiments and 4 cadre-regiments. The regiments are numbered from 1 to 14, and are divided into 4 squadrons (escuadron). The squadron is divided into 3 troops (seccion), and the troop into 2 half-troops (peloton), and 4 sections (escuadra).

The regiment may be on either the higher or the lower peace establishment. At the present time the majority are on the lower.

---

* "Ley Organica del Ejercito Nacional," 1900.
† "Reglamento para el Ejercicio de Tiro al Blanco," 1903.

*Squadron.**

Personnel.	Lower Peace Establishment.	Higher Peace Establishment.	War Establishment.
First-captain	1	1	} 1
Second-captain	1	1	
Lieutenants	3	3	2
Second-lieutenants ...	3	3	2
First-sergeant	1	1	1
Sergeant (assistant First-sergeant)	1	1	1
Sergeants	8	8	6
Corporals	12	12	12
Billeting corporal ...	—	—	1
Trumpeters	4	4	4
Shoeing-smith	1	1	1
Troopers	78†	114†	114†
Total	113	149	135
Horses	105‡	141‡	140‡
Mules	8	8	8

One trooper of each squadron is rated "Soldado de primera," and receives 1 dollar per month extra pay.

One half-troop§ in each squadron is organized as a "sapper section," and carries the following tools on one of the ammunition mules :—3 picks, 3 shovels, 3 axes, 3 crow-bars, and 3 screw-drivers. Three pairs of wire-cutters are carried by the sergeants.

* "Ley Organica," 1900.

† On the Peace Establishments 4 troopers are employed as teamsters. 2 as stretcher-bearers, and 6 as officers' servants. On the War Establishment the corresponding numbers are 4, 4, and 6.

‡ Does not include officers' chargers.

§ Captain Garcia y Pérez agrees with this statement, but asserts elsewhere that the sapper section consists only of a section with 2 picks, 2 shovels, 1 axe, 1 crowbar, 2 screw-drivers, and 1 pair of wire-cutters.

*Regimental Staff.**

Personnel.	Lower Peace Establishment.	Higher Peace Establishment.	War Establishment.
Colonel	1	1	1
Lieutenant-colonel	1	1	1
Major	1	1	1
First-captain, adjutant ...	1	1	1
Second-captains, assistant-adjutants	—	—	2
Second-lieutenants, orderly officers	2	2	2
First-sergeants, farriers ...	2	2	2
Corporal, shoeing-smith ...	1	1	1
First-sergeant, trumpeter	1	1	1
Sergeant, trumpeter ...	1	1	1
Corporal, ,, ...	1	1	1
First-sergeant, saddler ...	1	1	1
Second-class artificer, armourer	1	1	1
Corporal in charge of teamsters	1	1	1
Teamsters	5	5	5
Orderlies	3	3	4
Total	23	23	26
Horses	17†	17†	18†
Mules	10	12	12

Cadre-regiment.—The 4 cadre-regiments are numbered from 1 to 4. They are maintained either "in cadre" or on the lower peace establishment.

In the former case they consist of only 2 squadrons, each having an establishment of :—*

* "Ley Organica," 1900.
† Does not include officers' charges.

Personnel—

1 Second-captain.
3 Lieutenants.
2 Second-lieutenants.
1 First-sergeant.
1 Sergeant (assistant-first-sergeant)
6 Sergeants.
6 Corporals.
1 Artificer.
3 Trumpeters.
54 Troopers.*

Total 78

71 Horses.
6 Mules.

The regimental staff consists of :—†

1 Lieutenant-colonel.
1 Major.
1 First-captain, adjutant.
1 First-sergeant, farrier.
1 First-sergeant, trumpeter.
1 Corporal, trumpeter.
1 Corporal shoeing-smith.
1 First-sergeant, saddler.
1 Second-class artificer, armourer.
1 Corporal in charge of teamsters.
1 Teamster.

11

9 Horses.
5 Mules.

* Of the troopers, 2 are employed as teamsters and 6 as officers' servants, &c.

† "Ley Organica," 1900.

Each squadron "in cadre" is divided into 6 sections, each of 9 men, one of whom is termed the "soldado de primera," and receives extra pay at the rate of 1 dollar per month.

A cadre-regiment on the lower peace establishment is in every respect identical with a regiment of the line.

Mobilization.—It has already been mentioned that, on mobilization, the line regiments increase the number of their squadrons to 6, while the cadre-regiments each form a regiment on the higher peace establishment.

The following details show roughly the manner in which the change is carried out:—

Of the 4 second-captains, 2 take command of the newly-formed squadrons and the other 2 join the regimental staff as assistant-adjutants. The peace establishment of subalterns is sufficient to meet the demands of mobilization. 12 sergeants become first-sergeants, 6 corporals become sergeants, and 30 troopers become corporals. By this means 6 sergeants and 12 corporals are provided for each squadron. Each old squadron gives up 12 troopers who, with the non-commissioned officers, form nuclei of trained men.

The strength, then, of a regiment at war establishment is as follows:—

—	Officers.	N.C.O.'s and Men.	Horses.	Mules.
Regimental staff	8	18	18*	12
6 squadrons	30	780	840*	48
Total	38	798	858*	60

* Does not include officers' chargers.

Armament.—The trooper is armed with a sword and with a 7 mm. Mauser carbine carried in a bucket on the off-side behind the knee, or slung across the back at drill. The Lüger "Parabellum" pistol is to be issued in 1906. 65 rounds of ammunition per man per annum are allowed for practice.*

A certain number of explosive cartridges is carried in the squadron. In peace time the charge consists of 100 grammes of dynamite on a base of "kieselguhr" containing anything over 75 per cent. of nitro-glycerine. In time of war it is altered to 90 grammes of picric acid.

In either case, it is contained in a tin envelope 5½ inches long, 1½ inches wide, and 1 inch thick. The whole weighs about 4 ozs. At the upper end of the envelope is a small aperture closed by a wooden plug. This is removed and replaced by a detonator when it is desired to prepare the cartridge for action.

Equipment.—On the saddle is carried a dark blue saddle-cloth edged with red. On either side is a saddle-bag with a horse shoe strapped outside it. The lasso hangs on the off-side. The great coat is rolled and carried across the pommel. The blanket and a roll of clothing in a linen cover are carried across the cantle.

The saddle is of the Mexican pattern with a flat seat between a high pommel and a slightly lower cantle. The stirrup leathers are long and very broad; the irons are broad, but are not hooded. The single girth is of webbing and is fastened to a large ring directly under the pommel. The bit is severe. It has a long port and the curb-chain is replaced by a ring. The headstall and the bridle are separate. There is no snaffle and the bridoon pulls merely against the noseband.

All saddlery is of black leather.

---

* "Reglamento para el Ejercicio de Tiro al Blanco," 1903.

Uniform.—The uniform and distinguishing marks are described on p. 76.

V.—ARTILLERY.

The artillery is the most highly favoured arm, and the recent addition of 144 modern long-recoil Q.F. guns has rendered it by far the most formidable branch of the service.

The field artillery consists of :—

(*a*) 64 Schneider-Canet 75 mm. (2·95-inch) Q.F. guns. This is the present armament, but it will be retained only for the horse artillery.

(*b*) 48 St. Chamond-Mondragon 75 mm. Q.F. guns. These are now in store and will be the future field artillery armament.

(*c*) 48 De Bange heavy 80 mm. (3·15-inch) Q.F. guns converted to the Mondragon system. These are now in store and form the reserve for mobilization.

The mountain artillery consists of :—

(*a*) 48 De Bange light 80 mm. Q.F. guns converted to the Mondragon system.

(*b*) 24 Mondragon 70 mm. (2·76-inch) guns purchased in 1898.

(*c*) 6 B.L. mortars (80 mm.).

A portion of the present mountain artillery armament is to be handed over to the Light Artillery, which now consists of 16 1-inch Hotchkiss and 2-inch Nordenfeldt guns.

The machine-gun company is included in the corps of artillery, but it will accompany the infantry on service. It consists of 2 divisions, each of 12 guns. The one is of 7 mm. (0·28-inch) Colts, the other of Hotchkiss guns of the same calibre.

The coast artillery consists of ancient guns—many of them bronze—at the few coast fortresses.

Each battery is allowed 240 rounds per year for practice.

Horse Artillery.

The regiment of horse artillery consists in peace time of four 4-gun batteries. On mobilization the number of batteries is increased to 6.

The regimental staff, which is not increased on mobilization, consists of :—*

1 Colonel.
1 Lieutenant-colonel.
1 Major.
1 First-captain, adjutant.
2 Second-lieutenants, assistant-adjutants.
1 First-sergeant, trumpeter.
1 Sergeant, trumpeter.
1 Corporal, trumpeter.
2 First-sergeants, farriers.
1 Corporal, shoeing-smith.
2 Second-class artificers, armourers.

Total 14

8 Mules.

* "Ley Organica," 1900.

*Battery.**

Personnel.	Peace Establishment.	War Establishment.
First-captain	1	1
Second-captain	1	1
Lieutenants	3	2
Second-lieutenants	1	2
First-sergeants	1	1
Sergeants	6	5
Corporals	8	4
Gunners	24‡	32‡
Trumpeters	3	3
First-sergeant of drivers ...	1	1
Sergeant of drivers	1	1
Corporal of drivers	1	4
First-class drivers	10	10
Second-class drivers	16†	16
Shoeing-smith	1	1
First-sergeant, saddler ...	1	1
Collar-maker	1	1
Total	70	76
Saddle horses...	47	50
Draught horses	24	63

On either establishment the battery consists of :—

4 guns.
8 ammunition wagons.
1 battery wagon.
1 forge wagon.
2 supply wagons.

Two guns or 2 wagons are termed a section. Each wagon is drawn by 4 horses. The harness, with its

* "Ley Organica," 1900.
† 7 gunners and 2 drivers are detailed as orderlies, &c.
‡ 5 gunners are detailed as orderlies.

rope traces and pole-draught, is very similar to our own. It is of black leather.

The gun detachment consists of 1 sergeant, 1 corporal and 6 gunners. Two of the latter are rated as 1st-class gunners and receive 1 dollar per month extra pay.

The gunners are at present armed with a sword and revolver. The Lüger "Parabellum" pistol is shortly to be issued to all artillerymen. Both gunners and drivers are equipped similarly to the cavalry (p. 31).

The uniform and distinguishing marks are described on p. 76.

The following are some of the details of the 75-mm. Schneider-Canet gun :—*

Gun—	
Material	Steel.
Length, total	72·84 inches.
Weight	5 cwt. 1 qr. 20 lbs.
Bore { diameter	2·95 inches.
Bore { length	68·53 ,,
Rifling { system	Uniform.
Rifling { twist	6°.
Rifling { length	58·52 inches.
Number of grooves	24.
Muzzle velocity	1,476 f.s.
Firing mechanism	Percussion.
Number of rounds possible per minute ...	23.
Ammunition—	
Nature	Fixed.
Weight of filled shrapnel	11·02 lbs.
,, fuze	1·05 ,,
,, bursting charge	2·5 oz.
,, cartridge	2·27 lbs.
,, charge	12·3 oz.
Number of bullets	174.
Weight of bullet	154 grains.
Number of rounds in gun limber	30.
,, wagon limber ...	30.
,, ,, body	44.
,, per gun carried with the battery	178.

* The above dimensions are those of the experimental Schneider-Canet tested in 1901. They are contained in the "Memoria del Estudo Comparativo de los Canones Schneider-Canet y Mondragon," 1902, and are believed to be in the main correct.

Carriage—

Maximum length of recoil	... ...	31·1 inches.
,, angle of elevation ...	... ...	15·5°.
,, ,, depression	... ...	5°.
,, ,, traverse ...	... ...	2° right and left.
Diameter of wheel	... ...	48 inches.
Weight of ,,	... ...	147·2 lbs.
,, gun and carriage ...	... ...	10 cwt. 2 qrs.

Limber and wagon—

Weight of limber, without ammunition	...	8 cwt. 1 qr. 17 lbs.
,, ammunition wagon filled	...	28 cwt. 0 qr. 23 lbs.

The breech-block is on the interrupted-screw system, and is provided with safety arrangements for both travelling and loading. The recoil is taken up by 4 buffers underneath the gun. Of these, 2 are filled with glycerine and 2 with air compressed to 114 lbs. per square inch. The compression is effected by means of an ordinary motor-tyre pump. The ¼-inch steel shield is bullet-proof at 250 yards. The upper portion slopes towards the rear and the lower portion is hinged so as to be raised when on the march. The upper portion of the sighting slot is closed by a movable shutter. The gun and wagon limbers are identical. They consist of a single box, of which the rear opens to form a table. The shells are carried fuzed, and are packed horizontally, base to the rear. In the centre are 3 small boxes, 1 for the fuze-setter, the others for the sights and small stores.

Field Artillery.

There are two regiments of field artillery. Each consists of a regimental staff and of four 6-gun batteries.

On mobilization the regimental staff remains unchanged, but each regiment doubles the number of its batteries. The necessary officers are obtained from the military college, while gunners are supplied by the infantry, and drivers by the cavalry.

Regimental Staff:—*

1 Colonel.
1 Lieutenant-colonel.
1 Major.
1 First-captain, adjutant.
2 Second-lieutenants, assistant adjutants.
1 First-sergeant, trumpeter.
1 Sergeant, trumpeter.
1 Corporal, "
2 First-sergeants, farriers.
1 Corporal, shoeing-smith.
2 Second-class artificers, armourers.

14 Officers and men, with 6 horses.†

* "Ley Organica," 1900.
† Does not include officers' chargers.

*Battery.**

Personnel.	Peace Establishment.	War Establishment.
First-captain	1	1
Second-captain	1	1
Lieutenants	4	2
Second-lieutenants	2	2
First-sergeant	1	1
Sergeants	9	7
Corporals	12	8
Gunners	30	36
Trumpeters	3	3
First-sergeant of drivers ...	1	1
Sergeants of drivers... ...	1	1
Corporals of drivers... ...	6	6
First-class drivers	22	34
Second-class drivers... ...	32	21
Shoeing-smith	1	1
First-sergeant, saddler ...	1	1
Collar-maker	1	1
Total	128	127
Saddle horses...	15†	114†
Draught mules	54	122

The battery consists of :—

6 Guns and limbers.
12 Ammunition wagons.
1 Forge wagon.
1 Battery wagon.
2 Supply wagons.

The vehicles are drawn by mules.

The black-leather harness is similar to our own.

The gun detachment consists of a sergeant, a cor-

* The strength of a battery actually seen included 7 officers, 11 sergeants, 18 corporals, 125 gunners, and 30 drivers, with 15 horses and 72 mules.

† Does not include officers' chargers.

poral, and 4 gunners. Two of the latter are rated as "first-class gunners" and receive 1 dollar per month extra pay. The remaining gunners march with the wagons and are used as orderlies and to keep up communication with the guns.

All sergeants and trumpeters, the farriers, and the shoeing-smith are mounted. They and the drivers are equipped similarly to the horse artillery. The gunners are armed with the Remington carbine, which will be replaced by the Lüger pistol.

The uniform and distinguishing marks are described on p. 76.

*Details of the 75-mm. St. Chamond-Mondragon gun:—**

Gun—	
Material	Steel.
Weight...	6 cwt. 1 qr. 17 lbs.
Rifling	Increasing from 1° 30′ to 7° at 3 or 4 calibres from the muzzle, and thence uniform.
Number of grooves	32.
Firing mechanism	Percussion.
Muzzle velocity	1,640 f.s.
Length of recoil	60 inches.
Number of rounds possible per minute...	22.
Ammunition—	
Nature	Fixed.
Weight of filled shrapnel	14·3 lbs.
Number of bullets	278.
Weight of bullet	154 grains.
Bursting charge	2¼ ozs.
Charge...	21·16 oz.
Number of rounds in limber	36.
" wagon limber ...	36.
" " body... ...	54 or 64.
" per gun carried with the battery	216 or 236.

* The details are those of the 1901 model described in the "Memoria del estudio Comparativo de los Cañones de 75 mm. Schneider-Canet, St. Chamond-Mendragon, y Krupp, 1904." They are believed to be in the main correct.

Carriage—

Height of axis of gun	3 feet 5 inches.
Maximum angle of elevation	$17\frac{1}{2}$°.
" depression	5°.
" deflection	3° right and left.
Wheels { diameter	4 feet 4 inches.
Wheels { track	5 "
Weight of gun and carriage	20 cwt. 0 qr. 18 lbs.
Limber, filled with ammunition	15 cwt. 2 qrs. 23 lbs., or 14 cwt 2 qrs. 21 lbs.
Wagon body, filled with ammunition ...	23 cwt. 1 qr. 25 lbs., or 19 cwt. 2 qrs. 21 lbs.

With the exception of the eccentric Mondragon breech-block and of the recoil arrangement, the weapon is very similar to the French field gun. The single buffer is filled with oil and contains 2 Ehrhardt-pattern springs to return the gun to the firing position. The firing arrangement consists of a trigger, from which a lanyard is led along the trail and back round a block to a gunner sitting on a saddle attached to the off-side.

The shield is of $\frac{1}{5}$-inch steel. The upper portion is turned backwards over the gun, the lower portion is hinged so that it can be raised when on the march. The gun and wagon limbers are interchangeable. The wagon is placed alongside the gun in action and is tilted up on end, the bottom being iron-plated to form a shield. The perch is hinged. The fuze-setter takes 2 shells at a time, and is similar to the one in use in France.

Details of the 80-*mm. Converted De Bange gun*:—

The old 80-mm. (3·15-inch) De Bange gun has been converted to the Mondragon system by the addition of an eccentric breech-block, of a recoil buffer and recuperating springs, of a shield, and by the lengthening of the trail. The muzzle velocity and the weight of projectile have been reduced, and the ammunition is now of the "fixed" type. Otherwise, the original gun and carriage have been used, and the limbers and wagons are altered only in that the ammunition boxes have been improved. The shield is $\frac{1}{5}$ inch thick, and the lower portion is hinged to fold up when on the march. The sighting is telescopic and is constructed on the principle of the goniometre. The fuze-setter is of the French pattern.

Weight of gun and limber	35 cwt. 1 qr. 20 lbs.
Muzzle velocity	1,690 f.s.
Weight of shell	13·5 lbs.
Pressure in bore	11 tons per square inch.
Number of rounds possible per minute	30.

MOUNTAIN ARTILLERY.

On the peace establishment there is only a single regiment of mountain artillery, consisting of a regimental staff and of four 6-gun batteries.

On mobilization, the regiment doubles the number of its batteries and the regimental staff is divided up.

*Regimental Staff.**

Personnel.	Peace Establishment.	War Establishment.	
		1st Regiment.	2nd Regiment.
Colonel	1	1	—
Lieutenant-colonel	1	—	1
Major	1	1	—
First-captain, adjutant ...	1	—	1
Second-captain, paymaster	1	1	—
Second-lieutenants, assistant-adjutants	2	1	1
First-sergeant, trumpeter...	1	1	—
Sergeant, trumpeter ...	1	—	1
Corporal, trumpeter ...	1	1	—
First-sergeants, farriers ...	2	1	1
Corporal, shoeing-smith ...	1	—	1
Second-class artificers, armourers	2	1	1
Total	15	8	7
Horses	6	3	2
Mules			

* "Ley Organica," 1900.

*Battery.**

Personnel.	Peace Establishment.	War Establishment.
First-captain	1	1
Second-captain	1	1
Lieutenants	4	2
Second-lieutenants	4	2
First-sergeant	1	1
Sergeants	9	7
Corporals	13	8
Trumpeters...	4	3
Gunners	32†	36‡
First-sergeant, teamster	1	1
Sergeant, teamster	6	1
Corporals, teamster	6	6
First-class teamsters	6†	20
Second-class teamsters	12	30
Shoeing-smith	1	1
First-sergeant, saddler	1	1
Collarmaker	1	1
Total...	98	122
Horses	17	14
Mules	51	80

The gun detachment consists of a sergeant, a corporal and 4 gunners. Two of the last named are rated "first-class gunners" and draw one dollar per month extra pay. The remaining 2 corporals and 12 gunners are employed with the wagons or ammunition mules, while the spare sergeant acts as a connecting link between them and the battery.

The mounted men are equipped similarly to horse

* "Ley Organica." Another source gives the peace establishment of the battery as similar to that of a field battery, except that there are only 32 gunners, 42 mules, and *no* drivers.

† 6 gunners and 2 teamsters are employed as officers' servants, &c.

‡ 7 gunners are employed as officers' servants, &c.

artillery. The gunners carry a revolver, which is to be replaced by the Lüger "Parabellum" pistol.

The uniform and distinguishing marks are described on p. 76.

The battery is divided into:—

Battery	Baterie de Tir ...	6 guns with 24 mules. 48 an munition boxes on 24 mules.
	Echelon de Combat	36 ammunition boxes on 18 mules. Forge, boxes of tools, and farriers' stores.
	2nd line Transport.	Mules for supplies, forage, &c.

The Mexican pack-saddle (1900 pattern) is used for transport, and takes the portions of the carriage and the gun. The mules are led by chains attached to their halters.

The armament at present in use consists of the light 80-mm. converted De Bange, of the 70-mm. Mondragon, and of an 80-mm. mortar.

There are available only 24 mountain guns and 6 mountain mortars. It has been proposed to organize them into 6 batteries, each of 3 guns and 1 mortar.

Details of the 80-mm. De Bange-Mondragon Gun.

Weight of gun	231 lbs
" recoil cylinder	234 "
" wheels and axle	216 "
" front section of trail	246 "
" rear "	218 "
" gun and carriage	1,146 lbs.
Calibre...	3·15 inches.
Maximum pressure in bore	5·1 tons per sq. inch.
Muzzle velocity	853 f.s.
Remaining velocity at 3,000 metres (3,280 yards)	614 "
Weight of shell	13·5 lbs.
Remaining velocity of shrapnel bullets at 3,000 metres	902 f.s.
Number of rounds possible per minute ...	16.
" carried in the limber	18.
" " wagon body	24.
" per gun carried with the battery...	186.

This gun is similar to the converted field artillery

weapon in that it fires the same projectile and has the same sighting arrangements and fuze-setter. But it has no shield and its charge is smaller and its muzzle-velocity lower.

The limber has 3 boxes, each containing two 3-round carriers; the wagon body has 4 similar boxes.

The gun can be used either as a mountain gun or as a light field gun drawn by 4 mules, with a limber and 4 ammunition wagons.

In the former case the gun team carries the equipment in pack saddles, while the wagon is also carried in 4 sections.

Details of the 70 mm. (2·75 inches) Mondragon Gun.

Weight of gun	159 lbs.
Length ,, ...	39·3 ,,
Muzzle velocity	900 f.s.
Firing mechanism	Percussion.
Rifling { number of grooves ...	24.
Rifling { twist	Increasing.
Weight of shell	11 lbs.
,, charge	4½ ozs. with a 5-dram primer.

Details of the 80 mm. Mortar.

Weight of gun	154 lbs.
Length of bore	30 ,,
Weight of shell	13·5 ,,
Rifling { number of grooves	24.
Rifling { twist	Uniform.

Light Artillery.

In time of peace the squadron of light artillery, which is intended for use with the cavalry, consists of a regimental staff and of 16 light Q.F. guns and 16 ammunition wagons, each drawn by 4 horses.

On mobilization the staff remains the same, but the strength of the squadron is doubled.

Regimental Staff :—*

1 Major.
1 First-captain, for administration.
1 Second-lieutenant, adjutant.
1 Sergeant, farrier.
1 Driver, shoeing-smith.
1 First-sergeant, saddler.

—

6 with 3 horses.†

Squadron on Peace Establishment :—*

1 Second-captain.
2 Lieutenants.
3 Second-lieutenants.
1 First-sergeant.
8 Sergeants.
16 Corporals.
3 Trumpeters.
48 Gunners.‡
1 Sergeant of drivers.
8 Corporals „
24 First-class drivers.
32 Second-class „
1 Artificer.

—

Total 148

96 Draught horses.
78 Riding horses.

The gun detachment consists of a corporal and 3 gunners. The section of 2 guns is commanded by a sergeant, and the group of 2 sections by a subaltern.

The men are all mounted and are equipped similarly to the horse artillery. The gunners are armed with

* "Ley Organica," 1900. Another source gives the peace establishment of the squadron as—6 officers, 7 sergeants, 4 corporals, 3 trumpeters, 25 gunners, and 17 drivers, with 32 draught horses, and 15 riding horses.

† Does not include officers' chargers.

‡ 8 gunners are employed as orderlies.

sword and revolver. The latter is to be replaced by the Lüger "Parabellum" pistol.

The uniform and distinguishing marks are described on p. 76.

The present armament of 16 1-inch Hotchkiss and 2-inch Nordenfeldt guns is to be replaced by the 80 mm. De Bange-Mondragon mountain gun (p. 44).

The Machine Gun Company.

Though the machine gun company would always accompany and operate with the infantry, it is regarded as a portion of the artillery corps.

In time of peace it consists of 2 divisions, one of twelve 7-mm. (·275-inch) Colts, the other of twelve 7-mm. Hotchkiss guns. The Colts are on light two-wheeled carriages, the Hotchkiss guns are on tripods Either weapon can be packed on a single mule.

*Peace Establishment.**

Personnel.	Regimental Staff.	Division.
Officers	3	3
Sergeants	1	7
Corporals	—	12
Trumpeters	3 (Trumpeters, Gunners and Drivers together)	1
Gunners		28
Drivers		24
Total	7	75
Mules	—	25

On mobilization the strength is doubled; 20 horses are provided for the officers, and 101 mules for each of the 4 divisions.

* In August, 1905, the total strength was 6 officers and 100 men.

Each gun detachment consists of a corporal and 2 gunners. Two guns form a "section" under a sergeant, and 2 sections a "group" under an officer.

The men are armed with revolvers.

On service, 10,000 rounds per gun are carried on 4 mules; 12,000 rounds per gun per year are allowed for practice.

Fortress Artillery.

The fortress artillery consists of small detachments at Vera Cruz, Tampico, Mazatlan and Acapulco. The strength of each of them is :—

2 Officers.
1 Clerk.
3 Sergeants.
4 Corporals.
2 Buglers.
16 Gunners.
—
28

Artillery Train.

In time of peace the artillery train consists of a regimental staff and of 2 sections. The latter are employed in the transport of artillery stores in the city of Mexico.

Regimental Staff—

1 Major.
1 First-captain, for administration.
1 Second-lieutenant, adjutant.
1 Sergeant, farrier.
1 Corporal, trumpeter.
—
5, with 2 horses.*

* Does not include officers' chargers.

*Each Section**—

1 Second-captain.
2 Lieutenants.
1 First-sergeant, of drivers.
4 Sergeants, of drivers.
6 Corporal, of drivers.
15 First-class drivers.
25 Second-class drivers.
1 Shoeing-smith.
3 Trumpeters.
1 First-sergeant, saddler.

Total 59

10 Horses.†
138 Mules.

*Transport**—

4 S.A.A. wagons, each carrying 25,000 rounds.
13 Artillery ammunition wagons, each carrying 87 rounds.
1 Forge wagon.
1 Spare gun carriage.
1 Battery wagon.
3 Supply wagons.

Thus each section has a capacity of 100,000 rounds of S.A.A., and 1,131 rounds of gun ammunition.

Each wagon is drawn by 6 mules.

On mobilization the artillery train expands into as many divisional ammunition columns (Parque Divisionario) as may be necessary. Each of these

---

* "Ley Organica," 1900. Another source gives the strength of the section as 3 officers, 0 sergeants, 6 corporals, 2 trumpeters, and 31 men, with 16 riding horses and 216 mules.

† Does not include officers' chargers.

consists of a regimental staff, of 2 ammunition sections, and of an artificer section :—

Regimental Staff—*

1 Major.
1 First-captain, for administration.
1 Second-lieutenant, adjutant.
1 Sergeant, farrier.
1 Corporal, trumpeter.
3 Orderlies.
—
8, with 2 horses.†

Each Ammunition Section *—

1 First-captain.
2 Lieutenants.
1 First-sergeant, of drivers.
4 Sergeants, of drivers.
6 Corporals, of drivers.
20 First-class drivers.
30 Second-class drivers.
1 Assistant driver.
3 Trumpeters.
1 First-sergeant, saddler.
3 Orderlies.
—
Total 72
10 Horses.†
168 Mules.

Artificer Section *—

1 Second-captain.
1 Lieutenant.
25 Artificers.

---

* "Ley Organica," 1900. Another source allots 2 complete columns to each division.

† Does not include officers' chargers.

Transport of each Ammunition Section—

8 S.A.A. wagons.
13 Artillery ammunition wagons.
1 Forge wagon.
2 Spare gun carriages.
1 Battery wagon.
3 Supply wagons.

VI.—ENGINEERS.

The corps of engineers consists of :—

The Engineer Constructors.
1 Engineer Battalion.
1 Bridging Train.
1 Engineer Park.
1 Telegraph Company.

Engineer Constructors.

The corps of engineer constructors consists at present of 2 colonels, 6 lieutenant-colonels, 6 majors, 21 captains, and 20 lieutenants. In time of peace they are employed not only upon military duties, but also upon all manner of work for the civil departments. The employés are granted army rank and join the various units on mobilization.

Engineer Battalion.

The engineer battalion consists of a regimental staff and of 4 companies. Each company is divided into 3 sections, of which the first 2 are for general service (terraceros), and the third is for bridging.

*Regimental Staff**—

1 Colonel.
1 Lieutenant-colonel.
1 Major.
1 First-captain, adjutant.
1 Lieutenant, assistant-adjutant.
1 First-sergeant, trumpeter.
1 Corporal.
1 Sergeant.
4 Corporals.
8 Sappers, clerks.
1 First-sergeant, farrier.
1 „ „ saddler.

—

22, with 2 mules.

On mobilization it obtains a second-lieutenant as extra assistant-adjutant, a sergeant, 3 corporals, and 1 mule.

* "Ley Organica," 1900. Another source allots an additional officer to the regimental staff. This is probably a paymaster.

*Company.**

Personnel.	Peace Establishment.			War Establishment.		
	Staff.	Each of 1st and 2nd Sections.	3rd Section.	Staff.	Each of 1st and 2nd Sections.	3rd Section.
First-captain	1	—	—	1	—	—
Second-captain	1	—	—	1	—	—
Lieutenant	—	} 1 {	1	—	} 1 {	1
Second-lieutenant ...	—		—	—		—
First-sergeant	1	—	—	1	—	—
Sergeants	2	2	1	2	2	1
Corporals	1	7	2	1	7	2
Sappers	3	56†	12§	3	69‡	14§
Trumpeters	1	1	—	1	1	—
Sergeant, farrier	1	—	—	1	—	—
Total	11	67	16	11	80	18
Horses	4‖	2‖	1‖	4‖	2‖	1‖
Mules	1	3	5	2	8	21

* "Ley Organica," 1900. Another source gives the War Establishment as 6 officers, 184 N.C.O.'s and men, 9 horses, and 26 mules.

† On the Peace Establishment the 56 sappers consist of 40 sappers, 5 artificers, 8 teamsters, 2 stretcher-bearers, and 1 orderly.

‡ On the War Establishment, 3 artificers and 12 sappers are added. 6 sappers per company are officers' servants, and 12 are rated as first class sappers, and receive 1 dollar per month extra pay.

§ On the Peace Establishment the 12 sappers consist of 1 artificer, 10 teamsters, and 1 orderly. 2 teamsters are added on mobilization.

‖ Does not include officers' chargers. All the sergeants are mounted.

The general service sections carry the following equipment :—

90 Shovels.
120 Intrenching tools.
Dynamite.
Detonators.
Primers.
Electric leads.
Sketching instruments.
Flags and lanterns.

The 3rd section carries :—

Bridging material.
Canvas boat.
Steel cable (82 feet long and 1½ inches in diameter).
Coil of telegraph line.
12 iron dogs, in addition to those included in the bridging material.
Several coils of rope (200 feet long and ½ inch or 1 inch in diameter).

On mobilization one such company is allotted to each division. The new companies are formed by draughts from the cavalry for drivers and from the infantry for sappers.

The men are armed with the 7 mm. Mauser rifle and a bayonet.

The uniform and distinguishing marks are described on p. 76.

ENGINEER PARK.

The engineer park receives and issues stores, both in peace and in war. It consists of :—*

---

* "Ley Organica," 1900.

1 Colonel.
1 Lieut.-colonel.
1 major, for administration.
1 First-captain.
1 Second-captain.
2 Lieutenants.
1 Storekeeper (rank of first-captain).
1 First-sergeant, of drivers.
1 Corporal.*
12 First-class drivers.
1 policeman.

—

23, with 55 mules.

BRIDGING TRAIN.†

Personnel.	Peace Establishment.	War Establishment.
First-captain	1	1
Lieutenants	3	5
Storekeeper	1	1
First-sergeant	1	1
Sergeants	6	12
Corporals	9	17
Sappers	43‡	74‡
First-sergeant, farrier	1	1
" saddler	1	1
Shoeing-smith	1	1
Trumpeters	3	3
Policeman	1	1
First sergeant of drivers... ...	1	1
Sergeants of drivers	—	2
First-class drivers	8	27
Second-class drivers	12	27
Total	92	173
Horses	11	27
Mules	84	154

* 4 corporals are added on mobilization. † "Ley Organica," 1900.

‡ The 43 sappers include 4 shoeing-smiths, 2 carpenters, 2 collar-makers, 2 wheelers, 2 coopers. and 4 officers' servants. The 31 sappers added on mobilization include 2 shoeing-smiths, 2 carpenters, 1 stone-cutter, 1 collar-maker, and 4 stretcher-bearers.

On mobilization the train divides into bridging and divisional park sections. The former carries material for a 50-mètre (164 feet) bridge on 22 wagons, the latter also carries a 50-mètre bridge, and has 2 wagons for mining stores, 1 tool-wagon, 1 forge-wagon, and 1 wagon for dynamite and material for hasty demolitions.

The armament and equipment are similar to that of the infantry (p. 25).

The uniform and distinguishing marks are described on p. 76.

Telegraph Company.

In time of peace the telegraph company consists of a single section of 3 officers, with 16 telegraphists and linemen.

On mobilization additional companies are raised from the Government employés and one is attached to each division.

The company is to consist of a regimental staff and of 2 sections, the one with pack, the other with wheeled transport.

Personnel.	Regimental Staff.	Pack Section.	Wagon Section.
First-captain	1	—	—
Lieutenants	1	2	1
Sergeants	2	3	3
Corporals	1	4	7
Sappers	—	27	33
Trumpeters	4	—	—
Sergeant, farrier	1	—	—
Stretcher-bearers ...	6	—	—
Teamsters	—	11	12
Orderlies	9	—	—
Total	25	50	56
Horses	4	5	5
Mules	—	14	20
Wagons	—	—	6

The pack section carries :—

	mules.
10 miles of cable (88 lbs. to the kilometre)...	8
Instruments, battery, tent and flags ...	2
Stationery and equipment	2
2 sets of field instruments, battery and 1,640 feet of line	1
Supplies and forage	2

The wagon section carries :—

16 miles of bare wire (55 lbs. to the kilomètre).

250 iron posts, weighing 11 lbs. each, and in two 7 feet 3 inch joints.

25 iron posts, weighing 22 lbs. each and 21 feet long.

(These posts are placed 83 yards apart.)

The armament and equipment is similar to that of the infantry (p. 25).

The uniform and distinguishing marks are described on p. 76.

VII.—MEDICAL DEPARTMENT.

The medical department, of which the veterinary service forms a part, consists of :—

- Medical Officers.
- Administrative Officers.
- Apothecaries, with army rank.
- Veterinary Officers.
- A Company of Hospital Orderlies.
- An Ambulance Train.
- A Sanitary Park.

The officers are obtained from the military hospital and from the army medical school in the capital, and from other medical schools authorised by the Government.

A medical officer is attached to each regiment, battalion, and other similar unit. A veterinary officer is attached to each regiment of cavalry, battalion of artillery, and to the squadron of military police.

On mobilization a bearer company is attached to each division and field hospitals are established as required. Base hospitals are formed in the civil hospitals of the cities and the additional personnel is drawn from civilian sources.

Veterinary Service.—The veterinary service at present consists of 1 lieutenant-colonel, 6 majors, 12 captains and 6 cadets at the veterinary school, of which the lieutenant-colonel is president and 3 of the majors are instructors.

Hospital Orderlies.—The company of hospital orderlies is commanded by infantry officers, and has a peace establishment of :—

8 Officers.
35 Sergeants.
40 Corporals.
140 Orderlies.

Total 223

Ambulance Train.—The ambulance train is commanded by cavalry officers and has a peace establishment of :—

5 Officers.
1 First-sergeant, saddler.
1 „ „ of drivers.
6 Sergeants „
1 Sergeant, farrier.
12 Corporals, of drivers.
60 Drivers.

Total 86
8 Horses.
60 Mules.

It has 8 ambulances and 10 other wagons.

Sanitary Park.—The sanitary park consists of :—

1 Administrative officer.
2 Apothecaries.
3 clerks.
6 men.

Mobilization.—On mobilization the divisional bearer company is commanded by a surgeon-lieutenant-colonel and consists of 2 sections, each of the following strength :—*

* "Ley Organica," 1900.

4 Surgeon-majors.
4 Surgeon-lieutenants.
1 Ambulance officer.
19 Hospital orderlies.
7 fatigue men.
1 Sergeant, of drivers.
2 Corporals, of drivers.
6 First-class drivers.
6 Second-class drivers.

Total 50

The company equipment consists of :—

2 medical chests.
2 surgical chests.
2 operating tents.
2 sick tents.
2 officers' tents.
40 stretchers.
6 ambulance wagons.
2 supply wagons.

The field hospital consists of :—*

Personnel.	Medical Section.	Transport Section.
Surgeon-majors	6	—
Veterinary major	1	—
Apothecary captains	2	—
Captains	3	—
Lieutenants	1	2
Orderlies	67	—
Sergeant, farrier	—	1
Shoeing smith	—	1
Sergeant, of drivers	—	1
Corporal "	—	1
Drivers	—	32
Stretcher bearers	80	—
Fatigue men	10	—
Total	170	38

* "Ley Organica," 1900.

The equipment includes 20 stretchers, 26 tents, 12 baggage wagons, 2 supply wagons, 1 kitchen wagon and 1 wagon for medical stores.

Hospitals.

There are 11 army hospitals in Mexico, one at the capital and one at the headquarters of each military zone.

The medical school is carried on in connexion with the hospital in the capital and is the training place of the army medical service.

The director is a surgeon-colonel, and the staff consists of 7 surgeon-lieutenant-colonels and 3 surgeon-majors.

The hospital staff consists of :—

- 1 Administrative officer, with the rank of lieutenant-colonel.
- 1 Lieutenant-colonel.
- 1 Apothecary-lieutenant-colonel.
- 10 Surgeon-captains.
- 2 Apothecary-captains.
- 6 Civilian professors.
- 1 Dentist.

There are also several administrative officials, students doing duty in the dispensary and the laboratory, and 16 soldier orderlies.

The hospital has 700 beds, and an officers' ward to which officers are admitted at a small payment varying according to their rank.

The zone hospitals have each a staff of :—

- 1 Surgeon-lieutenant-colonel.
- 1 Apothecary.
- 1 Officer for administration.
- 1 Supply officer.

The most serious diseases are enteric, pleurisy, liver, pneumonia, tuberculosis and yellow fever. The mortality resulting from the three last amounts to between 34 and 44 per cent. of the cases.

VIII.—SUPPLY AND TRANSPORT.

Except in so far that regimental officers are appointed paymasters (habilidado) to their units, the pay and supply departments are almost entirely separated from the army. Supplies and forage are drawn from magazines controlled by the treasury, and this department appoints civilian paymasters (pagadores), who issue pay in time of peace and, in addition, conduct the whole system of supplies in time of war.

On mobilization these gentlemen—assisted by minor officials also appointed by the treasury—are posted to the larger units and become superior to the military supply officers. They are subject to military law and are responsible to the general officer commanding for all details of pay and supply. But their accounts are furnished direct to the treasury.

A column with 4 days' supplies is attached to each division or independent brigade and, as far as possible, is replenished by requisition on the local civil authorities.

The peace organization of the transport service consists of a regimental staff and of 2 companies.

Personnel.	Regimental Staff.	1 Company.
Lieutenant-colonel, commanding ...	1	—
Major, for administration	1	-
Captain	—	1
Lieutenants	1	2
First-sergeant, farrier	1	--
Sergeant, farrier	1	1
First-sergeant	—	1
,, saddler	—	1
Sergeants, of drivers	—	4
Corporal, trumpeter	1	—
,, of drivers	—	8
Shoeing-smith	—	1
Trumpeters	—	2
Drivers	—	40*
Total	6	61
Horses	3‡	10†
Mules	—	176‡
4-wheeled wagons	--	16
2- ,, carts	—	8

On mobilization the necessary number of similar companies is raised.

Mules.—Except in the horse artillery, mules are used for all army draught and pack work. Between 12·2 and 13·2 hands high, they are strong, hardy, and never sick or sorry. The majority are bred in Guanajuato and Jalisco. They cost between £6 and £12 a head.

Some 1,500 fitted with pack saddles are maintained in the army ready for mobilization.

The saddle consists of two thick pads, heavily quilted to prevent the tree bearing on the spine.

* From 2 to 5 drivers are employed as officers' servants, &c.
† Does not include officers' chargers.
‡ 40 mules are held as reserve.

It is provided with breast sling and breeching. A leather or rope surcingle passes over the whole load. Except that the mountain artillery has a special saddle, there is only one pattern for the whole army.

Donkeys.—Donkeys also are extensively used as pack animals. They would supplement the mule transport in time of war.

The donkey saddle is similar to that of the mule, except that it is smaller and is often without a breast sling. Pack animals are never linked together or led, but are driven in a herd by one or two men.

Wagons.—The army supply wagons are mostly of American make. They resemble the ordinary light farm wagons, with a tilt and a lock-under fore-carriage.

In the country districts much of the transportation is carried out by ox wagons or carts. The carts are either a substantial frame covered with a matting tilt, or resemble a Scotch cart with open framework sides. Oxen are used also for pack and saddle work.

Carriers.—In southern Mexico a considerable amount of transportation is undertaken by the Indians. The load of from 100 to 150 lbs. is carried on the back, and is slung from a broad leather belt across the forehead. The carrier wears only leather sandals and a pair of cotton breeches, but carries a blanket for the night. He eats little meat, yet he will march between 20 and 25 miles a day.

Note on Horses.—The supply of remounts is entrusted to one of the departments of the War Office, and no details are to hand as to the manner in which this duty is carried out.

The number of horses available in the country is estimated at 860,000.

The greater portion is bred in the northern States of Zacatecas, Durango, Chihuahua, Coahuila, Tamaulipas, Nuevo Léon, and San Luis Potosi.

They are spirited, active and enduring ; quiet and

easily broken. On the other hand, their quarters are weak and their action and jumping power are poor. Their feet are good, and they are seldom shod. Consequently the country blacksmiths are indifferent workmen. The animals are generally branded on the left flank with the mark of the "hacienda" they belong to. Their manes and tails are allowed to grow.

The Mexican travels at a walk and occasionally ambles or gallops. Consequently his horse does not know how to trot.

Their small stature—13·2 to 14·2 hands—renders them somewhat light for cavalry and horse artillery. Remounts are therefore purchased in Texas at the rate of £14 per head. This is some 3 times the price of the Mexican animal.

When travelling, the Mexican waters his horse in the morning and the evening, and gives him only a short drink at midday.

Forage consists of maize, barley, and chopped straw. Oats and hay are found only in the larger towns.

IX.—MILITARY POLICE.

The squadron of military police (gendarmeria del Ejército) is employed on provost duties both in peace and in war. Admission is restricted to men who have served their time in the regular army and left it with a good character, and to suitable men who are prepared to deposit a security to cover the expenses of their equipment. Preference is given to old soldiers. The men must be of good stature and constitution, able to read and write, and between 25 and 45 years of age. The term of enlistment is for 3, 4, or 5 years, and re-engagement is permitted.

On mobilization, additional squadrons are to be raised and detachments attached to the staffs of the higher formations. One half-troop under a second-lieutenant is to be attached to a brigade, one troop under a lieutenant to a division, and 2 troops under a second-captain to an army corps.*

The men are armed and equipped similarly to the cavalry (p. 31) except that they carry a revolver instead of a carbine.

Their uniform is described on p. 76.

The establishment of the squadron is† :—

Personnel.	Peace and War Establishment.
First-captain, of cavalry	1
Second-captain, of cavalry... ...	1
Lieutenants, of cavalry	3
Second-lieutenants, of cavalry ...	3
First-sergeant...	1
Sergeants	6
Sergeant, farrier	1
,, saddler	1
Corporals	12
Shoeing-smith	1
Armourer	1
Trumpeters	4
Troopers	84‡
Teamsters	2
Total	121
Horses	111§
Mules	10

* "Reglamento para el Servicio de la Gendarmeria del Ejército," 1898.

† "Ley Organica," 1900.

‡ 5 troopers are employed as officers' servants, &c.

§ Does not include officers' chargers.

President's Body-Guard.

To the military police may be added the President's body-guard which would release the regular troops who would be necessary for escort duty should the President ever take the field. It consists of :—

8 Officers.
4 Sergeants.
4 Corporals.
4 Artificers.
4 Trumpeters.
85 Troopers.

109, with 71 horses.

The men are carefully selected, principally from the cavalry and "Rurales." They must measure 5 feet 6 inches in their socks and be of robust physique. They must be able to read and write, know the four rules of arithmetic, and be prepared either to deposit a security of $100 or to submit to a deduction of pay until that amount is made good. They are enlisted for 2 years. They perform all escort duties, find the Palace guards, and orderlies for the various departments of the war office.

The uniform consists of a light blue tunic with white leather breeches. Knee boots are worn instead of the cavalry gaiter and ankle boot. The trouser stripe and cap band are light blue. The summer uniform is of white drill.

X.—FIRST AND SECOND RESERVES.

First Reserve.

It has been said that the First Reserve is composed of the officers in reserve and of the various bodies of Federal and State Police.

"*Rurales.*"—The country constabulary, known as the "Rurales," are organized on the lines of the "Guardia Civil" of Spain. They are under the Minister of the Interior (Home Secretary), but they may be described as the finest body of troops in the service of the Republic. They have served with great credit in the expeditions against the Maya and the Yaqui Indians, and have invariably responded to the trust reposed in them.

The rank and file are trustworthy, resolute, fearless men of the country farmer class. The officers are selected from the ranks.

The body is organized into 12 regiments, with a head-quarters at the capital consisting of a general officer with a small staff.

Each regiment consists of :—

1 Lieutenant-colonel, commanding.
1 Officer for administration.
1 Farrier.
15 Corporals.
200 Troopers.
———
218

Five of the regiments have their head-quarters in the larger towns of the Federal District. The 1st regiment has its head-quarters at Tlaxcala, the 3rd at Queretaro, the 5th at Tepic, the 7th at Pátzcuaro in Michoacan, the 9th in Tehuacan in Puebla, while the 11th and 12th, which were raised for the

Yaqui and Maya expeditions, are respectively at Guaymas in Sonora and in the Maya territory in Yuçatan.

The men are scattered about in small detachments and assist in maintaining order in the several States. They generally work in pairs, and their knowledge of the country, their endurance and their high sense of duty would make them excellent scouts in time of war.

The armament consists of a 13-mm. (·51-inch) Winchester carbine slung over the left shoulder by a baldrick and chain attached to the trigger-guard. Two revolvers, a knife, a short broadsword and a lasso are also carried. The stamped leather saddle is covered with silver mountings and the stirrups are large and heavy. A gaudy blanket is carried in a long roll over the cantle.

The men either provide their own horses, or purchase them from the Government by gradual payments. They receive 1 dollar, and a forage allowance of 30 cents., per day.

The uniform consists of the national or "Charro" costume. Full dress is a deerskin jacket and breeches, highly ornamented with braid and silver lace and buttons. The breeches are ankle-long and very tight. The enormous spurs are also highly ornamented. The headgear is the high broad-brimmed Mexican "Sombrero."

The working dress consists of grey cloth trousers and jacket, with which a white collar and a red tie are worn.

Federal District Police.—Like the "Rurales," the federal police are a responsible and well-disciplined body under the Minister of the Interior. They do no federal duty, and are responsible only for Mexico City and the vicinity. Their barracks are at Peredo in the capital.

They are commanded by an inspector with a staff

of 6 officers, and 32 officers and 16 sergeants doing duty at the city police stations.

They are divided into mounted and foot police The strength of the two bodies is :—

Personnel.	Mounted Police.	Foot Police.*
Senior officers	6	9
Junior „	21	72
Rank and file	401	1,820

The officers are all mounted. They are similar in quality and appearance to those of the army. They are armed with revolvers and sword. The mounted police always work in pairs. They have a long sword with brass hilt, and a carbine slung across the back. The dark blue great-coat is carried in a roll over the pommel, and a blue valise on the cantle. The blue saddle-cloth is marked with the letters G.M. (Guardia Municipal). The mounted police wear the long black cavalry gaiter with ankle boots. The tall shako is of black leather, and the cap lines and shoulder cords are white.

The foot police are armed with a revolver and with a truncheon. They wear a kepi, a hooded greatcoat, tunic, and trousers, all of dark-blue cloth. The back and sleeves of the tunic are ornamented with black braid.

Rural Federal Police.—There is also a special body of rural police for the country portion of the Federal Districts. It consists of 19 officers and 321 men.

Chapultepec Park Guard.—The Chapultepec Park guard is a small body of both mounted and foot police, who are quite distinct from the federal police, though their armament and equipment are the same. The

* According to the President's Message to Congress in 1905, the foot police is to be increased to a strength of 2,332.

mounted men are dressed in bottle-green, the foot police in grey.

State Police.—The police of the several States corresponds to that of the Federal District. But it is not of so high a quality, though it is quite as numerous in proportion to the amount of population. It is armed with truncheon and revolver. Its uniform is very similar to that of the federal police.

Fiscal Police.—The coast and frontier police are under the treasury. They are stationed at all the points of entry to the country, and amount to some 1,500 officers and men.

SECOND RESERVE.

As already stated, the Second Reserve consists of the National Guard of the several States. To it are appointed any regular or auxiliary officers who may be supernumerary after bringing the army up to its fighting strength. A special class of reserve officer is obtained by granting the rank of second-lieutenant to civilians who have passed medical and qualifying examinations.

Though the Corps of Invalids ("*Cuerpo Nacional de Invalidos*") belongs to neither reserve, it is inserted here for the sake of convenience.

It is limited to those men who—

(*a*) Have been wounded or otherwise rendered unfit for duty while on active service.

(*b*) Have no family or private means, and are over 60 years of age.

The invalids receive 25 cents. per day* and free uniform, medical attendance, &c.

* The "Reglamento del Asilo Militar de Invalidos" states that any pension to which the invalid may be entitled is raised to the rate of an infantry soldier's pay. The 25 cents per day is to cover incidental expenses such as washing, &c.

The staff of the institution consists of :—

1 General, or colonel.
1 Lieutenant-colonel.
1 Captain, for administration.
1 Lieutenant, adjutant.
1 Sergeant, bugler.
1 Corporal, bugler.
1 Porter.
6 Orderlies.
2 Male cooks.
2 Female cooks.

The corps may have a strength of 100 men. It consists of 2 companies, each divided into "active" and "decrepit" sections. The first category may be employed in time of war to relieve the regulars of the least fatiguing garrison duties. But the chief duty is to appear at the great State functions.

The strength of each company is at present :—

1 Captain.
3 Lieutenants.
2 Sergeants.
6 Corporals.
3 Buglers.
33 Men.

XI.—UNIFORM.

I. Officers.

Orders of Dress.—All officers wear a dark blue uniform. The trousers are the same in all orders of dress, but the tunic and headgear vary in the following particulars :—

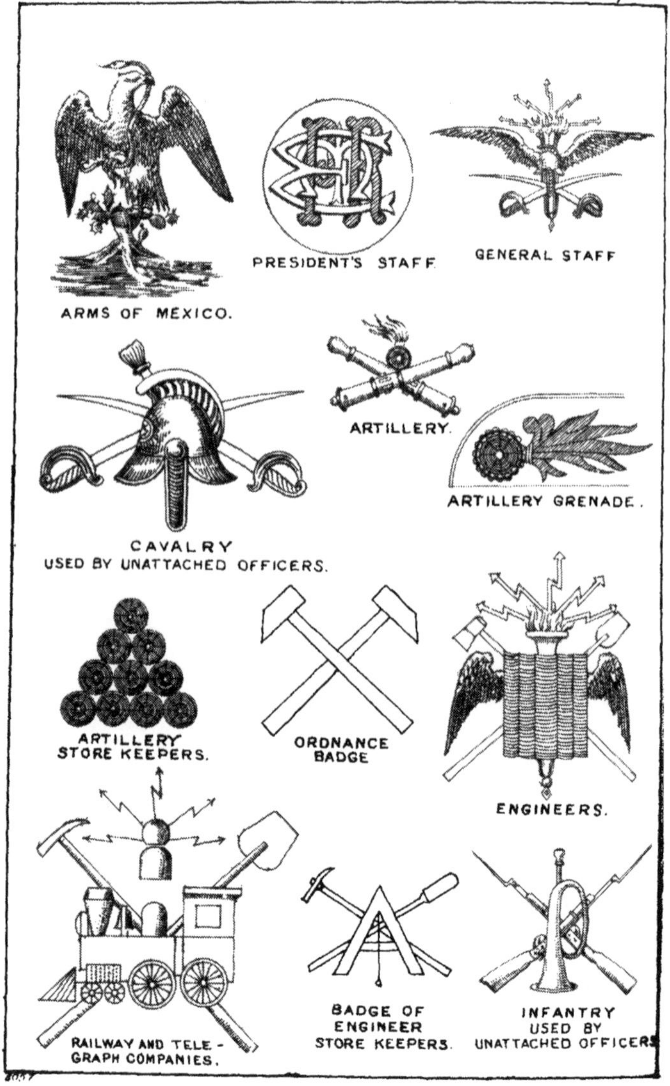

Departmental Badges.

To face p. 73.

ARMS OF MEXICO.

PRESIDENT'S STAFF.

GENERAL STAFF

ARTILLERY.

ARTILLERY GRENADE.

CAVALRY
USED BY UNATTACHED OFFICERS.

ARTILLERY
STORE KEEPERS.

ORDNANCE
BADGE

ENGINEERS.

RAILWAY AND TELE-
GRAPH COMPANIES.

BADGE OF
ENGINEER
STORE KEEPERS.

INFANTRY
USED BY
UNATTACHED OFFICERS

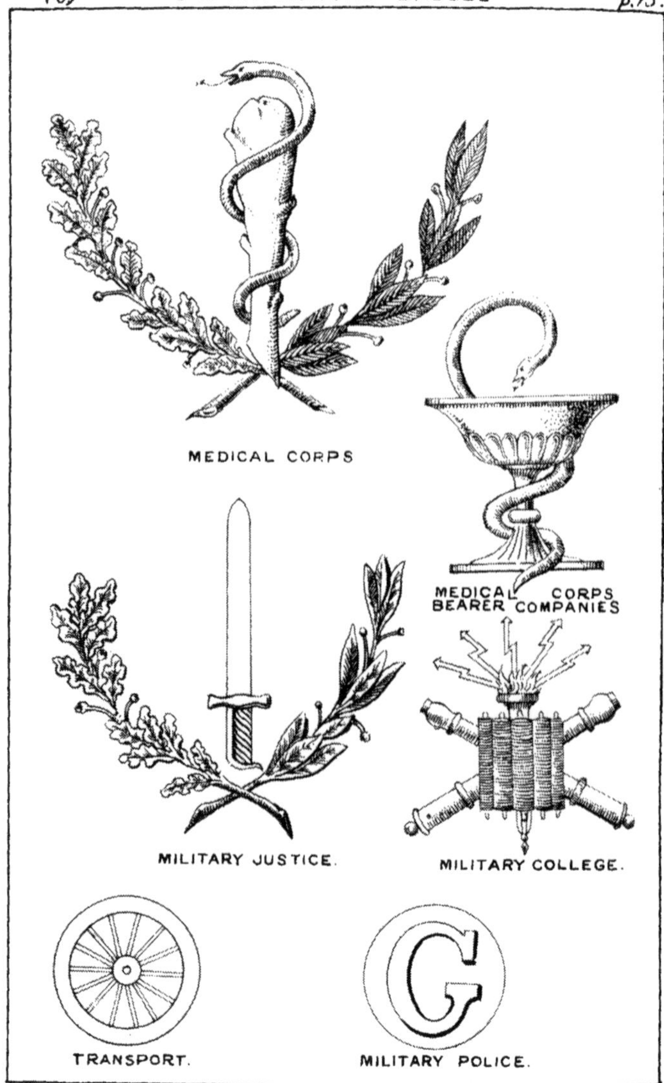

Weller & Graham. L^{td} Litho, London

Full Dress.—A tunic, black-braided in front and in rear, and with gold lace and facings on the collar and cuffs according to rank and corps. Headgear—a helmet, except for generals, who wear a low cocked hat trimmed with black plumes.

Dress.—A tunic, plain, but with full dress collar and cuffs. Headgear—a soft-topped flat cap with the badge and of the colour of the arm.

Undress.—A plain double-breasted frock with rows of brass buttons and with shoulder-straps. The dress cap.

Summer Dress.—Of white drill. A frock with brass buttons and pockets. Drill trousers and cap cover.

Greatcoat.—Plain dark blue cloth with hood and cape.

Saddlery.—The English hunting saddle with a saddle-cloth.

Armament.—A sword suspended from a black leather belt by a short steel chain sling. A revolver, carried loaded in a hip pocket in undress uniform, and in the belt in marching order.

Distinguishing Marks of Corps.—The various branches of the service are distinguished by the following differences :—*

(*a*) Badge of corps, as shown in the accompanying plates.

(*b*) Lace on collar and sleeves :—

Infantry	...	Gold.
Cavalry	...	Silver.
Staff	...	Gold, laurel leaf.

(*c*) Colour of facings and trouser stripe :—

Cavalry, Infantry, Transport and Military Police.†	Scarlet.

* "Reglamentos de Uniformes," 1898.

† The military police wear red braid across the chest and a single trouser stripe.

Staff, Engineers,* Artillery, and Military College.	Carmine, with a double trouser strip.
Medical Corps	Narrow gold trouser stripe.
Supply	Light blue.
Judge Advocate's Department.	The facing of the arm to which the officer belongs.

(*d*) Buttons :—

President's Staff... ...	Scientific Corps wear the badge of their arm. Cavalry and infantry officers wear plain buttons.
General Staff	Gilt, with the general staff badge.
Cavalry	Silver-plated, with the numeral of the unit. Officers of cadre-regiments wear plain buttons.
Infantry	Gilt, otherwise the same as cavalry.
Artillery	Gilt, with the badge of the corps.
Engineers	Gilt, with the badge of the corps.
Medical Corps	Gilt.
Military Police	Silver - plated, with a raised G.
Transport...	Silver-plated, plain.
Supply	Gilt, with a raised A.M.
Military College... ...	Gilt, with the inscription, "Colegio Militar."

* Engineers wear dark blue velvet collars and cuffs.

To face p. 75.

Shoulder Straps.

BRIGADIER.

GENERAL OF DIVISION.

Weller & Graham L^td Litho, London

COLONEL

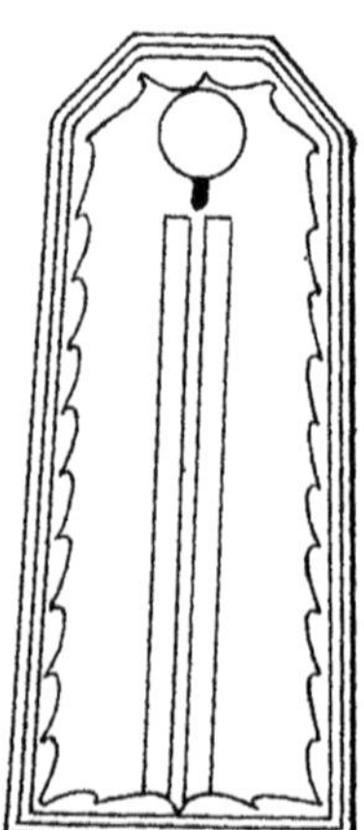

LIEUT. COLONEL.

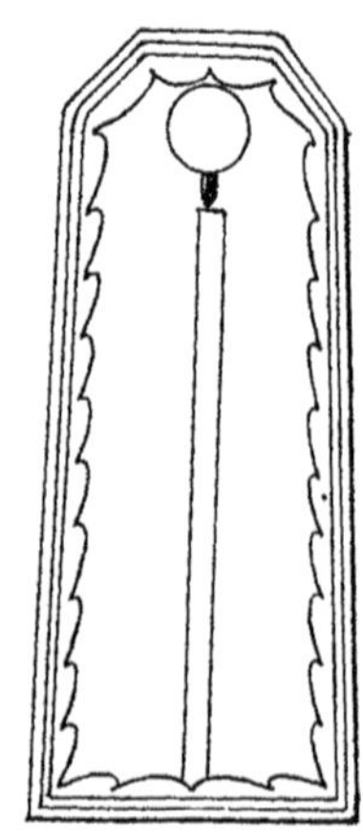

MAJOR.

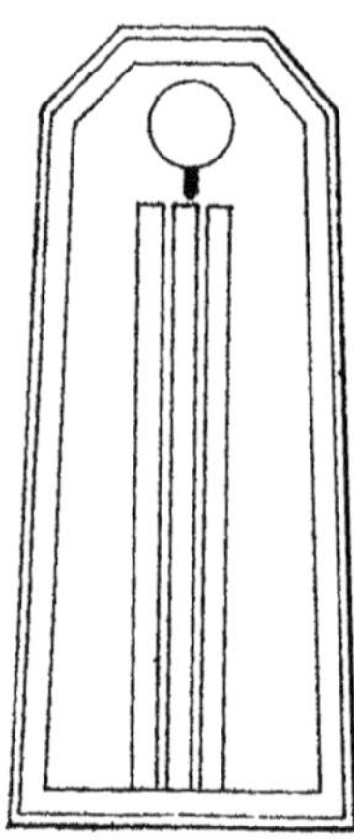

FIRST CAPTAIN.

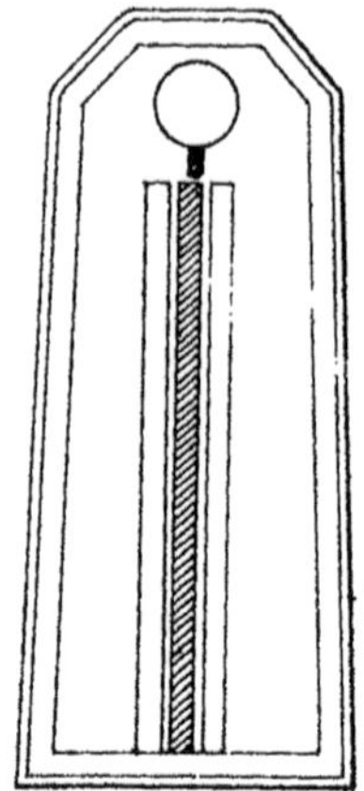

SECOND CAPTAIN.

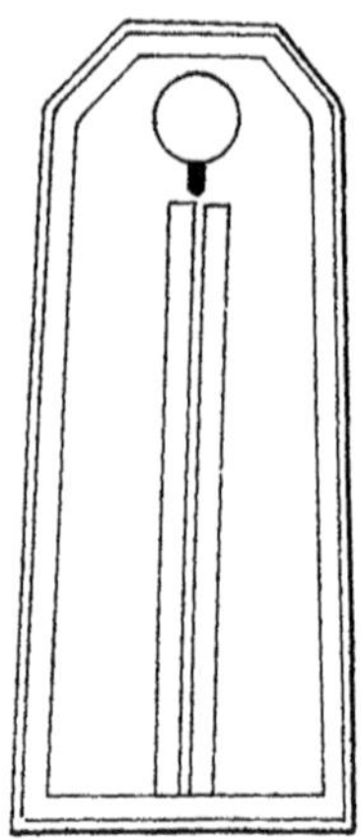

LIEUTENANT

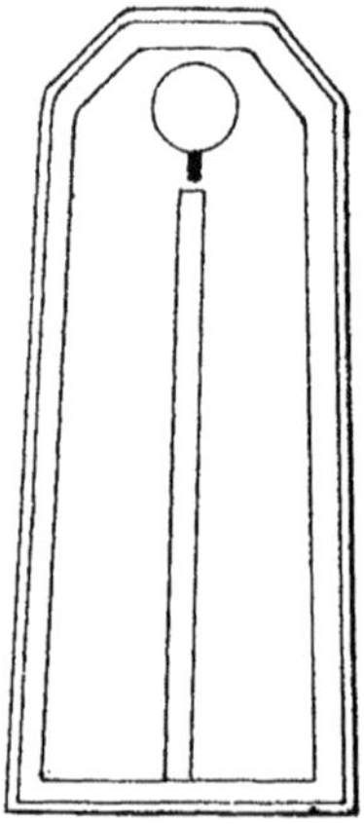

SECOND LIEUTENANT. 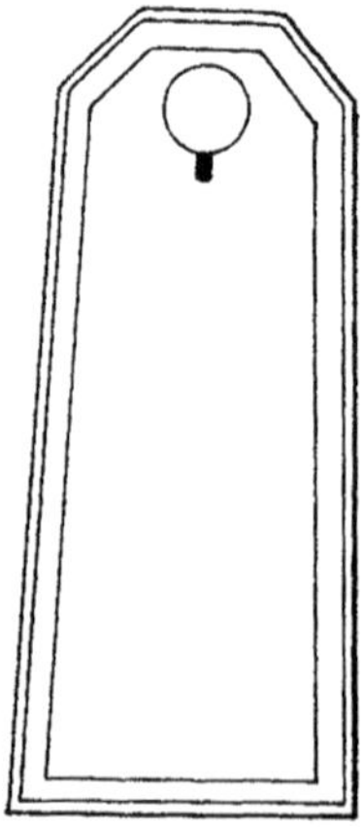 CADET. 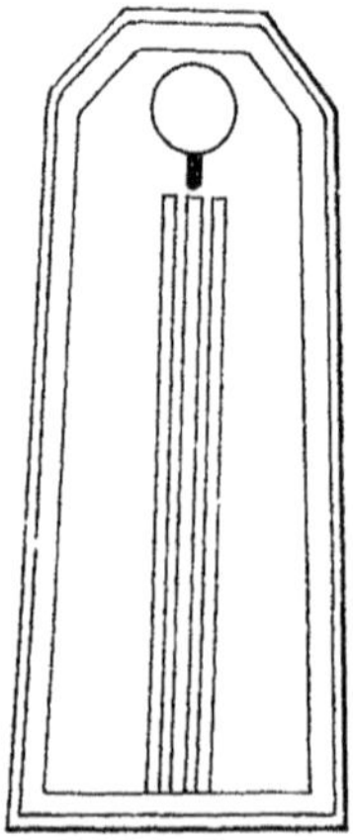 FIRST SERGEANT.

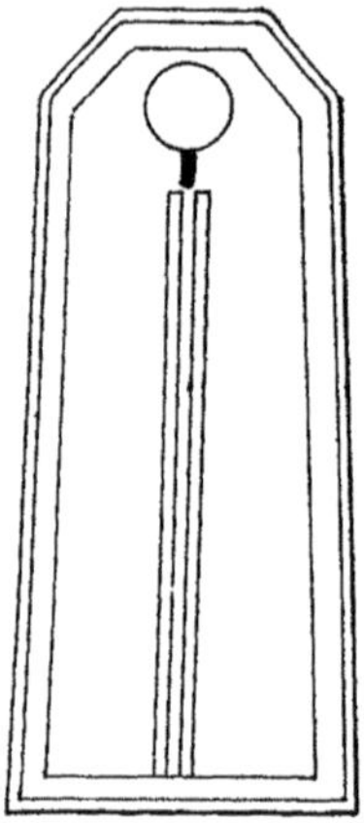

SERGEANT 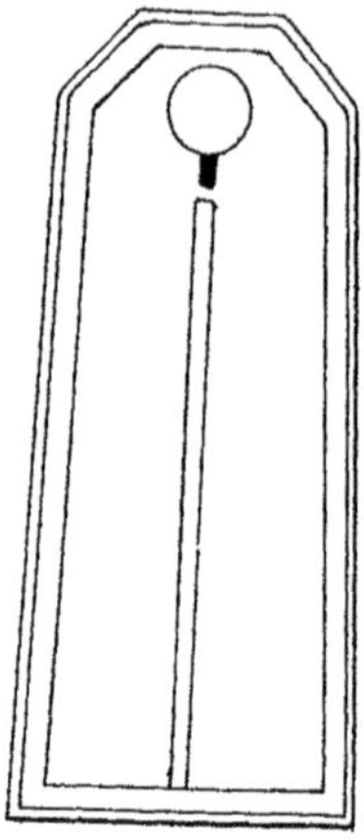 CORPORAL.

Weller & Graham Ltd Litho, London

Badges of Rank.—The following are the most easily distinguishable badges of rank* :—

General of Division ...	Heavily laced and fringed epaulettes. Badge: The Mexican Eagle between two silver-plated stars. Gilt spurs, with the inscription "Republica Méxicana."
General of Brigade ...	Similar to general of Division, except that the badge consists of the Mexican Eagle only.
Brigadier	The epaulette is replaced by a shoulder-strap with the Mexican Eagle as a badge.
Colonel	Laced shoulder-strap with a single star.
Lieutenant-Colonel ...	Laced shoulder-strap with two lines running lengthways.
Major	Laced shoulder-strap with single line.
First-Captain	Edged shoulder-straps with three lines.
Second-Captain	Edged shoulder-straps with three lines, the centre line being silver or gold, accordingly as the others are gold or silver.
Lieutenant	Edged shoulder-strap with two lines.
Second-Lieutenant ...	Edged shoulder-strap with one line.
Cadet of Military College	Edged shoulder-strap only.

* "Codigo Militar," 1900.

Men.

The uniform for the rank and file of every arm is of dark blue cloth. The shako is of the French pattern, and has a red pompom set in front. A soft-topped kepi is worn for drill and fatigue. The foot-gear is a light black boot, but leather sandals are generally worn by the infantry for marches and for drill. The mounted man wears a long black-leather buckled gaiter splayed over the instep.

The greatcoat is of dark blue cloth and has a hood. A "poncho," *i.e.*, a water-proof sheet with a hole in the centre, is also carried.

Drawers and shirts of cotton are worn under the uniform.

Distinguishing Marks—

(*a*) Colour of facings and trousers stripe :—*See* Officers, p. 73.

(*b*) Buttons and cap-badges :—

Infantry	Gilt buttons with the number or initial of the unit. Cap-badges with number or initial, the cadre-battalions bearing the letter C in addition. Regional battalions or companies bear on the cap-badge the letters B.R. or C.R.
Cavalry	Silver-plated buttons with the number or initial of the unit. Cap-badges also with the number or initial, the cadre-regiments bearing the letter C in addition.

Artillery	Gilt buttons with the corps badge. Cap badge, the corps badge.
Engineers...	As Artillery.
Medical Corps	As Artillery.
Supply	Gilt buttons with the letters A.M.
Transport...	Silver-plated plain buttons. Cap badge, the corps badge.
Military Police	Silver-plated buttons with a raised G. A similar letter in the cap-badge.

Badges of Rank.—The badges of rank consist of red stripes on a blue shoulder-strap and chevrons.

First-sergeant	Three stripes on shoulder-straps and chevrons.
Sergeant	Two stripes on shoulder-straps and chevrons.
Corporal	One stripe on shoulder-straps and chevrons.
First-class soldier ...	One chevron but no shoulder-straps.
Farrier or shoeing-smith	A horseshoe on the left arm.
Saddler	A cutting-tool on the left arm.
Artillery store-keepers ...	A pile of 10 round shot on the left arm.
Ordnance artificers ...	Two mallets, crossed, on the left arm.
Musicians	Two groups each of four bars on either arm.

PART II.

XII.—INTERIOR ECONOMY. PAY AND PENSION.

INTERIOR ECONOMY.

IN every branch or arm of the service the methods of interior economy are the same. In the regiment or battalion the colonel, the lieutenant-colonel and the adjutant have each a separate office. Their duties are mainly those of discipline and training.

The regimental paymaster is controlled by the treasury, from which he draws the necessary funds. He issues pay to the officers commanding companies, and is responsible for the financial transactions of the unit.

The major acts as second-in-command and controls the regimental stores and supplies. In this he is aided by the assistant-adjutants, each of whom has a separate office, the one for arms, accoutrements and clothing, the other for supplies.

The officers commanding companies draw their clothing and rations from the major and are responsible for its issue to their men.

The "Codigo Militar" lays down that inspections of all personnel and materiel are to be held at least once a month. The system of office work and returns is very similar to our own.

Court of Honour.—A noteworthy feature of regimental life is the Court of Honour (Junta de Honor). This is composed of the field officers of the unit and of one of the first captains. To all intents and purposes it draws up the "confidential reports," and also meets to decide whether the conduct of any officer affects the credit of the regiment.

Barracks.—The barracks are generally long, low buildings, single-storied except where there is a second floor over the front face. This front often contains the only entrance, usually a handsome gate with a strong officers' guard over it. The officers' guardroom occupies the one side of it, that of the men the other. In addition to the range of offices, there is a large, lofty whitewashed room for each company, squadron, or battery. Occasionally there is a spare room or verandah used as a dining room. The open-air kitchen is generally close at hand. The only furniture consists of a few forms, hooks, and shelves. The lower classes do not use beds, and thus the soldiers sleep on mats with a blanket for covering. The men wash themselves and their clothes in small stone troughs in the open air. The sanitary arrangements are somewhat primitive; otherwise the barracks are well kept and fairly clean. In mounted corps the saddlery is kept either in the barrack-room or in a separate store. The stables are half-open sheds with mangers to which the animals are fastened. Though roomy and airy, they are often badly paved and many stall partitions are either broken or altogether absent. They are usually built round three sides of a large yard, or "horse-run," containing a horse-bath and the drinking troughs.

There is generally a separate small yard for the sick horse stable and for the farrier's shop.

There are very few officers' quarters. The majority of them, as also the good-character men, sleep out with their families. The remainder of the personnel is practically confined to barracks.

Ration.—The daily ration consists of:—

Breakfast: Meat, coffee.
Dinner: Meat, rice, baked beans.
Supper: Baked beans, coffee.

But the women of the regiment are permitted to bring in the classes of food on which the lower orders of the country exist. This consists of tortillas (maize cakes), rice, beans, peppers and vegetables.

The beans take the place of meat and the maize-flour is more nutritious than that of wheat. Such food as this can be procured in every small country village—a fact which adds considerably to the mobility of Mexican troops.

PAY.

*Annual Rates of Pay:—**

Rank.	Cavalry.	Artillery.†	Infantry.
	Dollars.	Dollars.	Dollars.
Secretary of War and Marine...	—	15,001·50	—
General of division	—	6,000·60	—
" brigade	—	4,500·45	—
Brigadier	3,197·40	3,310·55	2,649·20
Colonel	2,774	2,838·75	2,555
Lieutenant-colonel	1,868·80	1,868·80	1,752
Major	1,697·90	1,697·90	1,551·25
First-captain	1,255·60	1,255·60	1,095
Second-captain	1,073·10	1,073·10	985·50
Lieutenant	890·60	890·60	857·75
Second-lieutenant	832·20	832·20	788·40
—			
First-sergeant, farrier	547·50	547·50	—
Sergeant, farrier...	438	438	—
First sergeant	365	365	365
Sergeant	273·75	313·90‡ 273·75§	255·50
Corporal in charge of baggage	284·70	—	270·10
Corporal	182·50	273·75‡ 182·50§	164·15
Drivers, first class	—	237·25	...
" second class	—	226·30	—
Private	164·25	164·25	138·70

* Captain Garcia y Pérez's report.

† Engineer and other rates of pay are similar to those of the artillery.

‡ Driver.

§ Gunner.

Owing to the large purchasing power of the monetary unit, these rates compare favourably with those of other countries.

Extra Pay.—As promotion in the staff and scientific corps is slower than in the line, extra pay at the following rates is granted to officers of these branches who may have completed one or more periods of *continuous* employment in the same rank.* It is withdrawn upon promotion, appointment to a tactical unit, or retirement.

				Dollars.	
5–10 years of employment...			...	180	per annum.
10–15	,,	,, ...	...	480	,,
15–20	,,	,, ...	...	720	,,
20 or more	,,	,, ...	...	1,200	,,

Non-commissioned officers and men receive 4 dollars for each year of their first term of service, provided that the period has been unbroken. They receive a similar amount on the completion of each term of re-engagement. Men disabled on service are considered to have completed their term. Those who re-engage receive a bounty of 20 dollars for a period of 4 years, one of 15 dollars for 3 years, and one of 10 dollars for 2 years.† The only conditions for re-engagement are that the man must be in robust health, and that he may not be over 45 years of age unless he be of exceptional physique.

In addition to the bounty, re-engaged men receive extra pay at the rate of 5 centavos per diem after 5 years' service. This is increased by as much again after every additional 4 years of service.

Decorations.—Officers and men receive long-service decorations.

Allowances.—Allowances are granted for washing and messing expenses.

---

* "Ley Organica," 1900.

† Captain Garcia y Pérez's report.

Pensions.—Officers and men retiring voluntarily after 20 years' service receive as pension half the pay of their last rank, provided that they held it for a period of at least 2 years.* After 25 years' service they receive two-thirds of the pay of their last rank, and after 30 years' service they may retire on full pay. Should they be compelled to retire by injuries received on service, they are promoted to the next higher rank and are then retired on the above conditions. Should the injuries be due to other causes, they receive half the pay of their last rank if they have less than 20 years' service, two-thirds of it after 20 years' service, and all of it after 25 years' service.

Pension is forfeited only by treason, or by a change of nationality.

XIII.—MANUFACTURING ESTABLISHMENTS—WARLIKE STORES.

The few military manufacturing establishments are all in or near the capital.

Arsenal.—The arsenal (Maestranza) repairs guns and carriages. It manufactures pack saddles, harness and, as far as possible, all artillery stores. It also makes wheels and wooden wagons. The museum and military library are attached to it.

The staff consists of :—

1 Director.
1 Assistant-director.
1 First-captain, in charge of administration.
Various technical officers and a staff of artificers.

The establishment is determined by the Minister of

* "Codigo Militar," 1900.

War. In August, 1905, it amounted to 8 officers and 85 men.

Arms Factory.—The arms factory (Fabrica Nacional de Armas) is in the same building as the arsenal. It converts Remington rifles to 7 mm. bore, makes spare parts of Mausers and repairs all small arms. It also manufactures friction tubes and small arm cartridge cases, filling them with powder and caps for the most part purchased abroad.

The staff is similar to that of the arsenal. In August, 1905, 7 officers and 100 soldiers and artifiers were employed.

Foundry.—The foundry (Fundicion Nacional) is at Chapultepec, 2 miles from Mexico. It repairs ordnance, and manufactures projectiles, fuzes, brass cartridge cases and the castings required by the other establishments.

The staff is similar to that of the arsenal. In August, 1905, it employed 7 officers, 62 ordnance artificers and a large number of civilian workmen.

Powder Factory.—The powder factor (Fabrica Nacional de Polvora) is situated 8 miles to the south-west of Chapultepec. It makes only black powder, and most of this is for commercial use. It also makes up dynamite cartridges, and gun ammunition from cases made in the foundry, and from shell made either there or in the iron foundry at Monterey.

The factory lies in a glen, and consists of a number of small buildings separated by traverses and connected by a tram line. Power is furnished by a large water-wheel. There are quarters for the officers and men, and testing laboratories well supplied with apparatus and machinery. On the adjacent hills are 3 separate magazines for storing the manufactured output. Explosions are frequent.

A commission has been appointed to study European methods with a view to establishing the manufacture of smokeless powder.

The staff consists of a colonel, a lieutenant-colonel, a major and 3 lieutenants, under whom are 60 artificers.

Artillery Depôt.—The artillery depôt (Almacenes Generales de Artilleria) is in the same building as the arsenal. It stores and issues all arms and ammunition for the army and all artillery matériel. It receives all warlike stores purchased abroad and holds them pending the decision of the Secretary of War.

Except that it has a major for administration, its staff is similar to that of the arsenal.

According to the "Ley Organica," 1900, 2 cadre-batteries for the assistance of the group of establishments are maintained with a personnel of :—

1 First-captain.
1 Second-captain.
6 Lieutenants.
1 First-sergeant.
12 Sergeants.
18 Corporals.
6 Trumpeters.
66 Gunners.
5 Store-keepers.
1 Clerk.
———
117

Clothing and Equipment Store.—The clothing and equipment store (Almacenes Generales de Vestuario y Equipo) is close to the arsenal, and the expense store is in the custom house (Aduana) buildings. Nearly all clothing and equipment is purchased by annual contract. The staff consists of :*—

* "Reglamento de los Almacenes Generales de Vestuario y Equipo," 1903.

1 Colonel, store-keeper.
1 Lieutenant-colonel, assistant.
1 Major, for administration.
2 Inspectors, appointed by the Treasury.
1 First-captain, secretary.
1 Second-lieutenant, clerk.
1 First-sergeant, door-keeper.
6 Sergeants.

WARLIKE STORES.

The amount of artillery matériel available has been enumerated on p. 32. Large quantities of ammunition have been secured with each consignment of guns purchased in Europe.

Of small arms there appear to be available :—

(*a*) 25,000 11-mm. Remington rifles, 1897 pattern ; 18,000 of these have been converted to take the 7-mm. Mauser cartridge.
(*b*) 72,000 7-mm. Mauser rifles, 1898 model.
(*c*) Many thousands of large-calibre Mauser rifles used by the State Guards.
(*d*) 7,000 13-mm. Remington carbines used by the artillery.
(*e*) 26,000 7-mm. Mauser carbines used by the cavalry.

In addition to the ammunition made up in the arms factory, many million rounds of smokeless powder cartridges have been purchased abroad.

The pistols at present in use are either Colt, or Smith and Wesson, or Remingtons of 11-mm. calibre. Officers also purchase the Belgian " Browning" double-barrelled pistol, or the Colt automatic revolver. All these will be replaced by the Lüger " Parabellum."

XIV.—EDUCATION.

Officers.

*Military College.**—The principal educational establishment is the military college in the Castle of Chapultepec. Youths from every class of society are admitted to it, the only conditions being that they must :—

(1) Be Mexican by birth or by naturalisation ;
(2) Pass an entrance examination ;
(3) Have the consent of their parents or guardians ;
(4) Have been vaccinated ;
(5) Be between 16 and 20 years of age, or between 15 and 20 if the sons of officers.
(6) Serve in the regular army for 4 years if appointed to cavalry, artillery, or infantry, or for 7 years if appointed to the scientific branches ;
(7) Should they leave the college or army before this period, either voluntarily or involuntarily, they must repay the expense incurred by Government on their behalf at the rate of 16 dollars per month. Before entering the college they must find a surety for this contingency.

During the first 3 years the course consists of the principles of the 3 arms, military law, mathematics, geography, history, English, freehand drawing, gymnastics, swimming, fencing and pistol practice. As far as possible the classes are limited to 25 pupils. During the first year the cadets are attached to infantry units for a period of 14 days,* during the second year to cavalry and during the third year to artillery. They perform the duties of second-

* "Reglamento del Colegio Militar," 1904.

lieutenants under the instruction of an officer of the unit. Immediately after each of these attachments they join a manœuvring force of all arms for another 14 days.* The senior cadets act as officers, the remainder form one or more companies. At the conclusion of these first 3 years the less promising cadets are weeded out and receive commissions as second-lieutenants or lieutenants, according to their merits, in the cavalry, the artillery, or the infantry. The more intelligent cadets also receive commissions as second-lieutenants, but are kept on for another 4 years to qualify for appointment to the general staff or to the scientific branches. During this period they are not paid as officers, but receive a small allowance. They are known as "Tenientes Alumnos" or as "Alumnos Pensionados." At the conclusion of the 5th year the more efficient receive commissions as lieutenants and a small increase of allowance. The course of instruction includes all professional and technical subjects, French, German and military hygiene. On the completion of the 7th year of instruction they are appointed lieutenants or second-captains, according to their merits, but they do not at once join their corps or units. The general staff officers spend some 10 months with the geographical survey, while the engineers and ordnance officers are employed on Government works and on technical duties. They are by now so highly trained in civil engineering and surveying that many of them either forfeit their surety or resign their commissions as soon as their compulsory term of service is at an end.

The administration of the college is very similar to that of Woolwich and Sandhurst.

---

* "Decreto del Presidente," 4th April, 1905.

The staff consists of :—

1 General or Colonel, director.
1 Colonel or Lieutenant-colonel of staff, engineers, or artillery, assistant-director.
1 Major, for administration.
1 Lieutenant, adjutant.
1 Medical Officer.

The educational staff comprises a very large number professors and instructors, both military and civil.
The cadets are divided into 2 companies, each of :—

1 First-captain.
1 Second captain, of staff, engineers, or artillery.
3 Lieutenants " " "
1 First-sergeant.
5 Sergeants.
10 Corporals.
4 Buglers.
10 First-class Cadets.
116 Cadets.

Each company has a large staff of servants and grooms, and 25 horses.

The director is immediately under the Secretary of War. The assistant - director is responsible for discipline, and supervises the training, both theoretical and practical. The medical officer delivers lectures on hygiene in addition to his other duties. The officers in charge of companies are responsible for the efficiency of their commands, and are also professors in a military subject, while the company lieutenants are instructors.

The first-class cadets correspond to the sergeants and corporals of Sandhurst. The cadets sleep in large dormitories of from 50 to 60 beds, and feed together in a large dining room. They are well cared for, discipline is strictly maintained and they appear to be happy and contented.

Holidays are limited to 1 week in March or April, and to about a month in December. Even for urgent private affairs not more than 1 week in the year may be granted and even that amount must be sanctioned by the Secretary of War.

Probationers' School.—For the reasons already mentioned on p. 7, the probationers' school (Escuela Militar de Aspirantes) was founded in 1905 as a complement to the military college. It is located at Tlalpam, near the capital.

Its immediate objects are :—*

(1) To provide subaltern officers for the cavalry, artillery and infantry branches.

(2) To prepare for the rank of officers those sergeants who have passed a preliminary professional examination in their units.

(3) To form a school of instruction for all present officers below the rank of major who have not been through the military college.

The permanent staff consists of :—

1 Major or Lieutenant-colonel, commandant.
1 First-captain, for administration.
16 Professors and Instructors, in addition to the company officers.
1 Second-lieutenant, adjutant.
1 Surgeon-major.
3 Clerks.
5 Soldier servants.

The provisional establishment of probationers is 95. They are divided into 3 sections or companies, according to the arm they select on entering the school.

---

* "Reglamento Provisional de la Escuela Militar de Aspirantes," 1905.

Personnel.	Cavalry.	Artillery.	Infantry.
First-captain	— }	1	{ 1
Second-captain	1 }		{ 1
Lieutenant	1	1	1
Orderlies	3	3	3
First-sergeant, probationer ...	—	—	1
Sergeants, probationers... ...	2	3	2
Corporals ,, ...	4	4	6
Corporal, standard-bearer, probationer	—	—	1
Probationers	26	12	36
Horses	32	—	—

The course of instruction lasts 1 year, in two terms of 6 months each. It comprises the tactics of the 3 arms up to regimental or battalion drill, the use and care of warlike stores and armament, the elements of field fortification, military law, sketching, and other professional subjects, mathematics, geography, history, gymnastics, fencing, riding and pistol practice.

At the end of this course the probationers and sergeants who pass a satisfactory examination are granted the rank of second-lieutenant in the *auxiliary* forces, and are attached to a regular unit of their arm for 12 months. At the end of this period they are examined by a board of officers and, should they be well reported on, they are granted commissions in the regular army and are ante-dated to their first appointment in the auxiliary forces.

Probationers.—The civilian candidate for admission must—

(*a*) Be of Mexican nationality.
(*b*) Be between the ages of 18 and 21.
(*c*) Have passed through an elementary school.

(*d*) Not have been expelled from the military college or from any other Government institution.

(*e*) Have been vaccinated and be of good physique.

The administration is similar to that of the military college. The youths wear officers' uniform without the badges of rank. They are paid 1½ dollars per day, but of this they receive only 1 dollar per day while attached to a r-giment or battalion, and 50 cents per week as pocket-money while they are at the school. The remainder is retained to feed and clothe them, and to provide them with a complete officer's outfit when they leave the school.

Should the probationer fail to pass the half-yearly examination, he drops a term. Should he fail twice, he is removed from the school and is compelled to serve for 5 years as a sergeant in the corps to which the Secretary of War may appoint him. Should he be badly reported upon by his unit, even after having passed successfully through the school, he may be removed from the service.

Sergeants.—Officers commanding units are permitted to recommend for commissions 1 first-sergeant per regiment or battalion, and 1 sergeant per squadron, battery, or company.

They must be under 25 years of age, have at least 6 months' service in their rank and be of exemplary character. Finally, they must have passed the examination held in the unit on the civilian probationers already attached to it. They are then admitted to the probationers' school and, except that they mess and live with the non-commissioned permanent staff, are treated in every way like the civilian probationers. Should they fail in two examinations they are sent back to their regiments to complete their term of service—the time spent at the school being forfeited—in their original rank.

Officers.—Of the army officers who have not been through the military college, 2 from each unit quartered in Mexico and 1 from every other unit will be sent to the probationary school for a course of instruction. Except by special arrangement they do not live in the school, but merely attend at the hours of instruction. Should they fail in the first-term examination, they are detained for another 6 months, and lose that amount of seniority. Should they fail in the second-term examination, or twice altogether, they are sent back to their regiments and are passed over until they have passed one of the subsequent school examinations.

School of Gunnery and Musketry.—The school of gunnery and musketry (Escuela de Tiro) was established in 1900, and was intended to train officers in the use of guns and small arms, in the manufacture of explosives and in practical military engineering. Every year there were to be 2 six-months' courses, each of 50 officers of all arms. No classes have been held recently, and much of the equipment has been transferred to the probationers school. The school is on the eastern outskirts of the capital, and consists of a group of buildings providing lecture rooms, gun sheds, a laboratory and a meteorological observatory. Between these and Lake Texcoco is the "Polygon," with a trial range for field guns and small arms.

Rank and File.

Elementary Schools.—Of recent years the Mexican Government has evinced considerable interest in the improvement of the rank and file, and in 1904 it published comprehensive instructions* upon the management of elementary military schools.

---

* "Reglamento para las escuelas de enseñanza primaria elemental." 1904.

One of these is established in every regiment or battalion, and in every considerable detachment absent from headquarters for any lengthy period.

The course lasts 3 years, and consists of reading, writing, arithmetic, geography, the most rudimentary elements of geometry, and national history. Except on Saturdays, Sundays and Saints Days, every man attends daily for between 1 and 2 hours. Examinations are held at the end of every year, and prizes are given, varying from 5 dollars to 50 dollars for a man who has done well in each of the 3 years.

The staff of each school consists of a headmaster with 2 assistants. The headmaster is either a regimental officer—preferably a graduate of the military college--in which case he receives extra pay, or a graduate at one of the State normal schools, in which case he is granted the rank and pay of a second-lieutenant of cavalry.

The assistants are sergeants.

The energies of the staff are stimulated by the fact that they also receive money rewards and are noted for further employment.

All these schools are under the Secretary of War, who appoints a sub-inspector-general as his representative. This official is responsible for the whole of the system of education and for the interior economy of the schools. He visits in person the schools of the Federal District once a week, and those of the distant States once a year.

Miscellaneous.—In addition to these elementary schools there are courses for farriers and shoeing smiths, and a school for trumpeters and buglers* which at present forms part of the school at Tlalpam.

This latter has a staff of 3 music masters (maestro de música), and the details under instruction are commanded by 2 captains and 2 lieutenants. The course

* "Reglamento para la Escuela de Bandas Militares," 1903.

lasts 5 months. Two second-lieutenants and 3 men are taken from each battalion of infantry and regiment of cavalry or artillery, 2 second-lieutenants and 2 men from each cadre formation and company of machine guns or artillery train.

XV.—MILITARY LAW.

The military law of Mexico is administered by the following bodies:—

(1) The Public Ministry of Military Law.
(2) The Supreme Military Tribunal.
(3) The Plenary Tribunal.
(4) The First Court.
(5) The Second Court.
(6) The Courts of First Instance.
(7) The Courts-Martial.

Public Ministry of Military Law.—Military law is administered by a department at headquarters known as the "Ministerio Publico Militar."* Its principal official, the "Procurador-General," corresponds to our judge-advocate-general. He must be over 35 years of age, and have been an attorney for at least 5 years. There are 2 assistant-procuradors and, on the application of the Procurador-General, the Secretary of War may appoint as many more as he considers advisable. Besides these, there is an assistant to each permanent judge of the Courts of First Instance, and such judges may themselves appoint additional temporary officials.

The duties of this department are:—

(1) To secure the equable and speedy administration of military law.

---

* "Ley de Organizacion y Competencia de los Tribunales Militares."

(2) To aid and secure the fulfilment of all rules and ordinances connected therewith.
(3) To represent and protect the public interests at courts-martial.
(4) And to ensure the execution of the decrees of those courts-martial.

Supreme Military Tribunal.—The supreme military Tribunal has jurisdiction over the whole territory of the Republic. It consists of :—

President, a general of division or of brigade.
Vice-President, a general of brigade.
6 Magistrates, generals of brigade or brigadiers.
3 Magistrates, civilians with corresponding military rank.
6 Clerks, 4 being officers and 1 a sergeant.

There are also 2 official "Defensores" or counsel for the accused.

Plenary Tribunal.—The above officials are all members of the plenary tribunal (Tribunal Pleno), which is the real executive body and which is divided into two courts (Primera Sala y Segunda Sala).

To be effective the plenary tribunal must consist of a minimum of 7 members of the supreme military tribunal. The "Procurador-General" is consulted at its sittings, but has no vote. Its duties are :—

(1) To decide questions on competency of jurisdiction raised in the courts of the supreme military tribunal.
(2) To hear charges against functionaries and employés of the department.
(3) To decide appeals against penalties inflicted on such functionaries or employés by the supreme military tribunal, by the first or second courts, or by the Procurador-General.

(4) To decide all points not especially entrusted to the supreme military tribunal, or to other courts.
(5) To acquaint the Secretary of War of all petitions for pardon or for commutation or reduction of sentence when this is not done by one of the other courts.
(6) To discuss doubtful points of law.
(7) To indicate to the Secretary of War any reform in military law conducing to the better administration of justice.
(8) To draw up and submit to the war office the regulations of the supreme military tribunal, with any necessary reforms.
(9) To supply the Procurador-General with criminal statistics.
(10) All matters dealing with the appointment and distribution of the personnel of the department

First Court.—The first court consists of the President, the two senior military members and the senior legal member of the plenary tribunal. Its staff consists of a lieutenant-colonel of infantry as secretary, and of 11 clerks, varying in rank between lieutenant-colonel and sergeant. Its duties are:—

(1) To determine the competency of courts of first instance.
(2) To try cases submitted by commanding officers.
(3) To revise all findings outside the competency of the second court.

Second Court.—The second court consists of the remaining members of the plenary tribunal, and has a similar staff.

Its duties, avoiding any trespass on those of the first court, are:—

(1) To deal with charges submitted by commanding officers.
(2) The revision of warrants, judicial sentences, &c.
(3) The revision of summary sentences by commanding officers or by courts of first instance.
(4) The revision of disciplinary punishments.

Courts of First Instance.—Under the supreme military tribunal there are 4 permanent courts of first instance in the Federal District, 2 in Vera Cruz and 1 in each military command. Others may be instituted wherever the exigencies of the service renders them necessary. Each Court has a judge, an "Asesor"—who corresponds to our judge-advocate, and a "Defensor."

Courts-Martial.—The above bodies may be said to constitute the staff of the military law department. In time of peace justice is administered by the "Consejo de Guerra ordinario," which corresponds to the district court-martial. It consists of a colonel as president, and of from 4 to 6 members, of whom only 2 may be as junior in rank as captains. Only military offenders come before it. Its power of punishment is unlimited. But the rules of procedure guarantee the interests of the prisoner, the defence has entire freedom and the proceedings are as brief as possible. The prisoner may have any soldier or civilian as "friend." There are also ten permanent courts-martial, 2 being in the Federal District and 1 in each military command. The members are detailed from their units for considerable periods.

The "Consejo de Guerra extraordinario" corresponds to our field-general court-martial. It is composed of 5 officers who may not be below the rank of captain and who should not belong to the same unit as the prisoner. It, too, has unlimited powers of punishment.

Commanding Officer.—The commanding officer has

power to inflict reprimand, or to place a field officer under arrest in his quarters for 24 hours. He may place other officers under arrest for 1 month, but if the term exceeds 15 days he must report the occurrence to his immediate superior. He can suspend sergeants or corporals for 1 month, and can place them and the men under arrest for the same period.*

Punishments.—The punishments consist of† :–

- Reprimand.
- Fine.
- Minor arrest (1 to 30 days).
- Major arrest (31 days to 11 months).
- Ordinary imprisonment (1 to 15 years).
- Extraordinary imprisonment (20 years).
- Suspension of appointment.
- Cashiering for officers ; discharge with ignominy for N.C.O.'s and men.
- Death.

These penalties are very similar to our own, but are inflicted in longer terms. Thus, even in peace time, a man who deserts while on sentry duty is punished with 6 years imprisonment, and the death penalty is frequently inflicted. Consecutive terms of arrest amounting to more than 1 year become ordinary imprisonment. One-half of the term of ordinary imprisonment may be redeemed by good behaviour, and one-third of extraordinary imprisonment, which latter is applied only instead of the death penalty. Imprisonment carries with it the loss of any appointment.

---

* "Codigo Militar," 1900.
† "Ley Penal Militar," 1901.

APPENDIX A.

Coinage.—By the monetary law of December 9th, 1904, the Mexican currency was based upon a gold standard. The unit is the dollar or "Peso." It is equivalent to 75 centigrammes of pure gold. Its value in English money is from 2*s.* 0½*d.* to 2*s.* 1*d.* It is divided into 100 centavos.

The coinage consists of :—

Gold ...	10 pesos, 5 pesos.
Silver ...	1 peso, 50 centavos, 20 centavos 10 centavos.
Nickel...	5 centavos.
Bronze...	2 centavos, 1 centavo.

*Regardless of the fact that the "real" (12½ centavos) has long since been called in, the term is still often used by tradespeople in quoting their prices. Thus 1½ dollars may be termed "un peso y cuatro reales."

Paper currency is limited to the notes of the National Bank of Mexico, the Bank of London, Mexico, and South America, and the State banks. The notes of the last named are often subject to slight discount beyond the limits of the State.

Weights and Measures.—The metric system of weights and measures was introduced on June 19th, 1895, and its use was enforced by the law of January 1st, 1904.

* Campbell's new revised "Complete Guide of Mexico," 1904.

The following old Spanish terms are still occasionally used :*—

Nature of Measure.	Mexican Term.	Metric Equivalent.	English Equivalent.
Square ...	Fanega ...	3·566 hectares	8·813 acres
" ...	Caballeria ...	42·795 "	105·75 "
Dry	Fanega ...	90·814 litres	2·498 bushels
"	Carga ...	181·629 "	4·996 "
Liquid ...	Cuartillo ...	0·456 "	0·805 pints
" ...	Galon ...	3·65 "	0·805 gallons
Avoirdupois ...	Onza	28·765 grammes	1·015 ounces
" ...	Marco ...	230·123 "	0·507 pounds
" ...	Libra... ...	460·246 "	1·015 "
" ...	Arroba ...	11,506·00 "	25·4 "
" ...	Quintal ...	46,025·00 "	101·5 "
" ...	Carga ...	138,074·00 "	304·4 "
" ...	Tonelada ...	920,493·00 "	0·906 tons
Long	Pulgada ...	0·0232 metres	0·916 inches
"	Pié	0·279 "	11·00 "
"	Vara	0·838 "	33 00 "
"	Legua ...	4,190·00 "	2·6 miles

Maps.—The best foreign map of Mexico appears to be the one published by the State Department, Washington, U.S.A., in 1900. It is on a scale of 50 miles to the inch.

The surveying section (Comision Geografica Exploradora) of the General Staff is now engaged on a map to the scale of 1 : 100,000. This is really a reconnaissance based on points fixed astronomically and not by triangulation. The map is reproduced by photo-zincography.

Sheets have been issued of the Federal District, of the States of Mexico, Morelos, and Puebla, of nearly all Vera Cruz, Hidalgo, and Tamaulipas, and of those portions of Sonora and Yucatan in which took place the expeditions against the Yaquis and the Mayas.

* "Statistician and Economist," 1905–6.

A large scale cadastral map of the capital and the surrounding country is now in course of preparation.

Individual States have issued maps of their own, but they are inaccurate and poor in execution.

Magnetic Variation.—The magnetic variation of the inland districts is not at present forthcoming. The following are taken from charts, and read from north to south on either coast :—

		Taken in 1893, and decreasing 1′ annually.
West Coast	... W. Coast of Lower California between latitudes 28° and 30°	11° 55′ E.
,,	... E. Coast of Lower California between latitudes 29° and 30°	12° E.
,,	... W. Coast of Lower California in latitude 26°	11° E.
,,	... S. of Lower California	10° E.
,,	... Intersection of longitude 108° and of latitude 23°	9° 40′ E.
,,	... Intersection of longitude 106° and of latitude 19°	8° 50′ E.

		Taken in 1895, and decreasing 3′ or 4′ annually.
East Coast	... N. of Laguna de Tamiahua	8° E.
,,	... Vera Cruz	7° E.
,,	... Tabasco, longitude 93°	6° E.
,,	... N. of Yucatan	5° E.

APPENDIX B.

VOCABULARY OF MILITARY TERMS.

Acemila ... ... Pack animal.
Alcance ... ... Range.
Almacen ... ... Shop, store.
Ametralladora ... ... Machine gun.
Arma de fuego ... ... Fire-arm.
Armon ... ... Limber.
Artilleria montada ... Field artillery.
„ de montaña ... Mountain artillery.
„ caballo ... Horse artillery.
„ de plaza ... Garrison artillery.
Artillero ... ... Gunner.
Asistente ... ... Orderly, officer's servant.
Avancarga ... ... Muzzle-loading.
Ayudante... ... ... Adjutant.
Basto ... ... Pack saddle.
Batallon ... ... Battalion.
Bateria ... ... Battery.
Brigada ... ... Brigade.
Caballo ... ... Horse.
Caballeria ... ... Cavalry.
Cabó aposentador ... Billeting corporal.
Cabo de banda ... ... Band corporal.
Camillero... ... ... Stretcher-bearer.
Capitán ... ... Captain.
Carga ... ... Charge.
Carro de municiones ... Ammunition wagon.
Cartucho ... ... Cartridge.
Clarin ... ... Trumpeter.
Cofre de municiones ... Ammunition box.
Columna ... ... Column.

Compania...	Company.
Conductor	Teamster, driver.
Corneta	Trumpeter.
Coronel	Colonel.
Cuadro	Cadre.
Cureña	Gun carriage.
Cureña de respeto ...	Spare gun carriage.
Cuartel General	Headquarters.
Cuerpo	Corps.
Deposito	Depôt.
Ejercito	Army.
Enfermero	Hospital orderly.
Equipo	Equipment.
Escolta	Escort.
Escuadra	Squad of infantry, section of cavalry.
Escuadron	Squadron.
Escuela	School.
Espoleta	Fuze.
Estado Major	General staff.
Estopin	Tube.
Explorador	Scout.
Fabrica	Factory.
Ferro-carril	Railway.
Forraje	Forage.
Fragua	Forge wagon.
Fundicion	Foundry.
Fusil	Rifle.
Ganado	Flock, establishment of animals.
Granada	Shell.
Granada de metralla ...	Shrapnel.
Habilidado	Regimental paymaster.
Hacha	Axe.
Herramiento	Tool.
Herrero	Shoeing-smith.
Infanteria	Infantry.
Ingeniero	Engineer.

Jefe ... ... Field Officer.
Machete ... ... Chopper.
Maestranza ... ... Arsenal.
Mancebo ... ... Shoeing-smith.
Mando ... ... Command.
Mariscal ... ... Farrier.
Major ... ... Major.
Mochila ... ... Knapsack.
Montaje ... ... Gun-mounting.
Morral ... ... Haversack.
Obrero ... ... Artificer.
Oficial ... ... Officer.
Pagador ... ... Paymaster.
Pala ... ... Shovel
Pareja ... ... Team of animals.
Peloton ... ... Half-troop of cavalry, half-section of infantry, gun detachment.
Peso ... ... Weight, dollar.
Pieza ... ... Gun.
Plana Major ... ... Regimental Staff.
Plantilla ... ... Establishment.
Polvora ... ... Powder.
Porta-guion ... ... Standard-bearer.
Portatil de zapa ... ... Portable intrenching-tool.
Racion ... ... Ration.
Reemplazo ... ... Substitute.
Retrocarga ... ... Breech-loading.
Rueda ... ... Wheel.
Saco de cebada ... ... Nose-bag, barley-bag.
Saco de ración ... ... Haversack.
Sargento ... ... Sergeant.
Seccion ... ... Troop of cavalry, section of infantry.
Servicio de Administracion ... ... Supply department.
Servicio de Sanidad ... Medical
Soldado ... ... Soldier

Subteniente	Second-Lieutenant.
Sueldo	Pay.
Talabartero	Saddler.
Tambor	Drummer.
Teniente	Lieutenant.
Teniente Coronel ...	Lieutenant-colonel.
Tienda	Tent.
Tiro	Round of ammunition.
Tren a lomo	Pack train.
Trenista	Driver.
Trompeta	Trumpeter.
Tropa	Troop.
Unidad	Unit.
Vivac	Bivouac.
Viveres	Provisions.
Zapador	Sapper.
Zapapico	Pickaxe.
Zona	Zone, military division

Appendix C.

FLAGS.

Appendix C.

FLAGS.

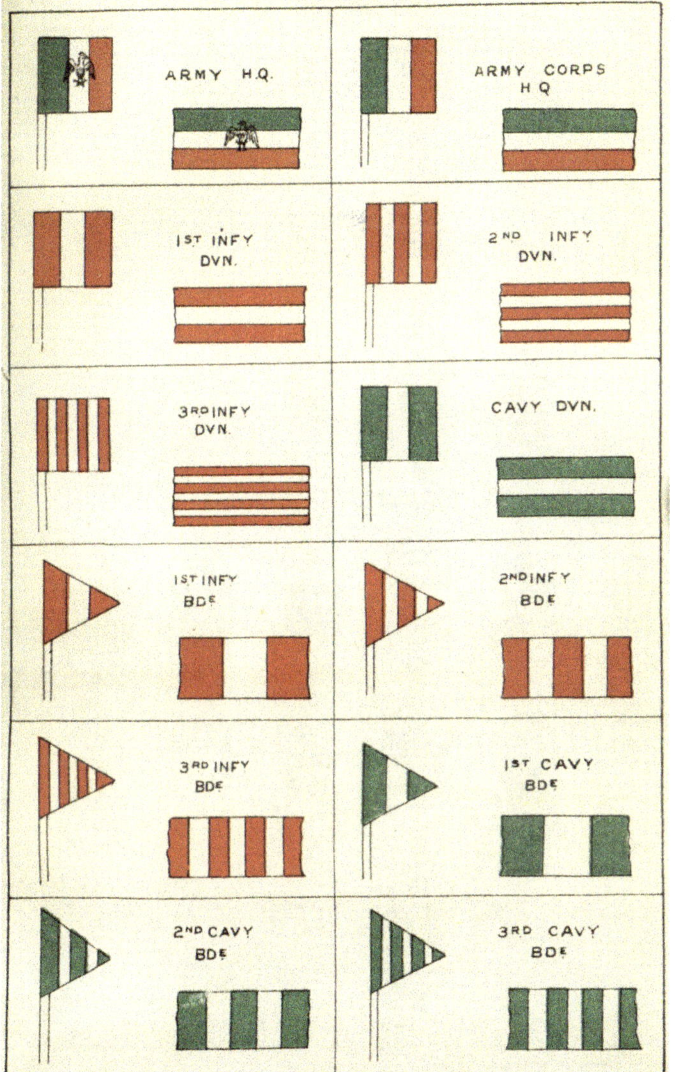

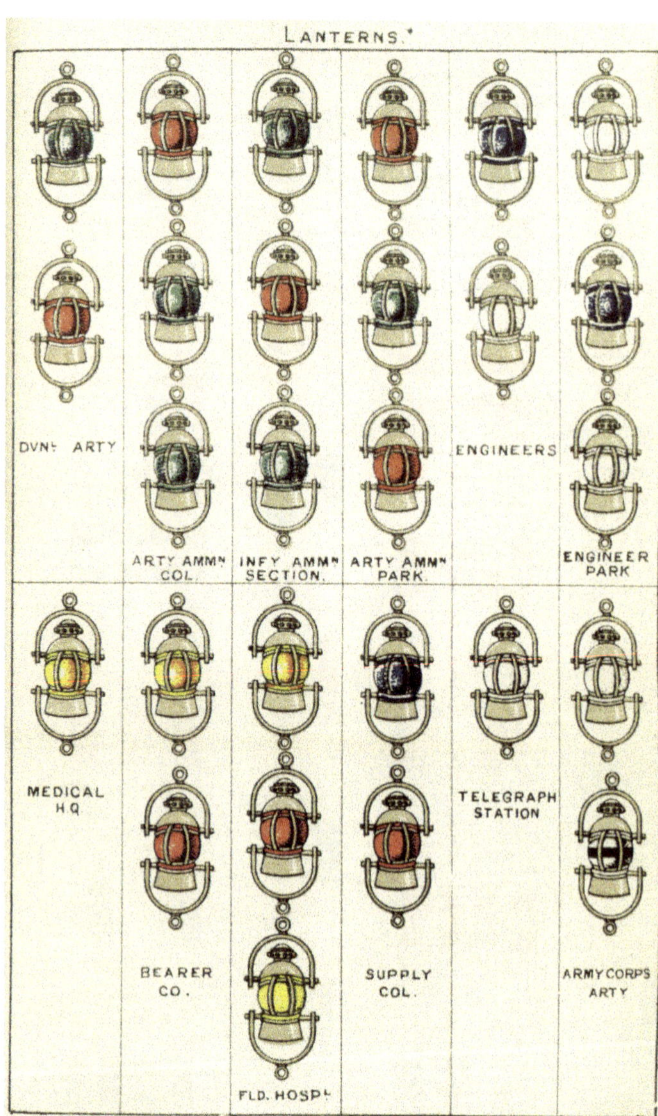

* *The lanterns are hung below one another as shown in the plate.*

Weller & Graham Ltd Litho London

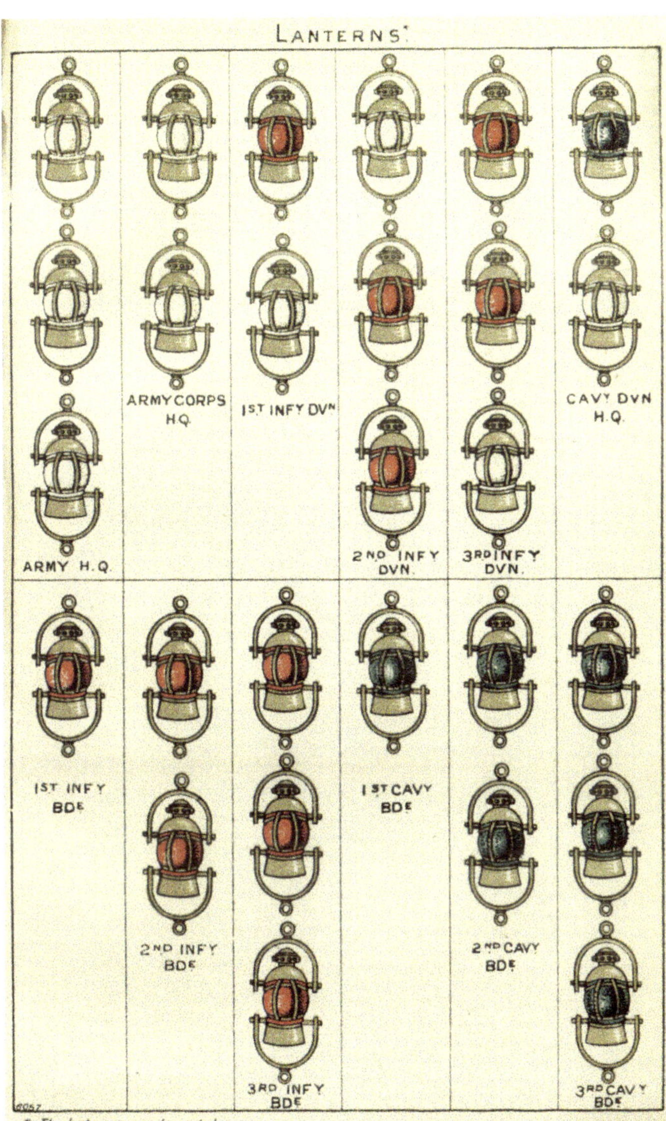

* The lanterns are hung below one another as shown in the plate.

www.ingramcontent.com/pod-product-compliance
Ingram Content Group UK Ltd.
Pitfield, Milton Keynes, MK11 3LW, UK
UKHW021835270726
14058UKWH00002B/165

9 781847 348432